Loving God's Way

LOVING GOD'S WAY

Discovering and Embracing Your Bone

KLAAS H BALOYI

PARTRIDGE
A Penguin Random House Company

Print information available on the last page.

To order additional copies of this book, contact
Toll Free 0800 990 914 (South Africa)
+44 20 3014 3997 (outside South Africa)
orders.africa@partridgepublishing.com

www.partridgepublishing.com/africa

PRESENTED TO:

_____

BY:

_____

DATE:

_____

CONTENTS

Acknowledgements

It was not long since I had an encounter with the Lord when He implanted in my spirit that I write this book. I still remember the feeling. Fired up from the joy of realising how much loved and honoured I was to can be entrusted with such a humbling opportunity to be used by God despite my not so admirable past. I owe it to the Almighty God, whom I first and foremost would like to thank for having assigned me the responsibility to write this book and for all the revelations. All praises and glory to Him for financing this book project and making it a success.

Secondly, sincere gratitude goes to my lovely and beautiful wife, Rachel. I am honestly and truly appreciative of all the love, time and support you afforded me during the period of writing this book. Your understanding as I utilised your precious time, which you and our two beautiful children deserved, is encouraging and much appreciated. I am truly honoured to have you as my bone, and you will forever remain my only true love until Jesus Christ returns.

Of course our little boy and girl, Nsovo and Kwetsimani, came into our lives at the time I had made some headways in writing this book. But the little, yet treasurable time I had been denying them, locking myself in a room to avoid their noise and disturbances at times, was also unjust. They too deserved quality time with their father. My sincere gratitude to them as well and I love and cherish them so much. To my parents, Elias and Elizabeth Baloyi, I put off my hat for you for honouring me as your first born son. How grateful I am that your love yielded something as wonderful as me. I will forever be grateful to you for having raised me to be the man I am today.

I also extent my gratitude to Bishop Solomon Mkhonza and his wife, Pastor Lindiwe Mkhonza. Your leadership, guidance and prayers have aided me to recognise the gift that the Lord has blessed me with, which I believe was further fanned by your teachings and parenting. I also thank all my friends, brothers and sisters in the Lord who supported me throughout this project. If space was permitting, I would mention all of your names here.

Special thanks to you, Derrick & Brenda Mashao for all your prayers and encouragements, you are such a blessing to me and my family. Your encouragement and motivation on this book project gave me strength to go all the way and made me believe in its successful completion. David and Annah Moepya, thank you for your prayers and motivation as well. Johannes Masombuka, you never stopped encouraging me to write this book, which you always saw as a need for relationships and marriages in the end-time church. Thank you very much for your support and encouragement.

To my dear sister in the Lord, Yvonne Mohamme, the journey you travelled with me in the past 12 years has been exciting and I have really thrived under your guidance and motivation. I really thank the Lord for you. You received me with warm hands when many of those I looked up to appeared alien to my situation at the time. The latter also goes to your wonderful husband Stephen Mohamme, affectionately known to many as malome "uncle". Thank you malome for your love and support as well. You have been such a wonderful role model to me. As much as this book is about love, I could not, secondary to God, have learned to love from another as I have from you. I do now realise why our paths crossed. I believe the Almighty introduced you into my life for purposes such as this. To teach me how a man should love and take care of his family.

Nomvula "Nomvi" Bulangwe. My sister. My friend. We did not just serve the Lord together, but have always been each other's keepers. May the Lord richly bless you in all your future endeavours. To my brother and friend Thapedi Peter Sesoko, you are the best and I believe the Lord raised us together for a purpose. Seeing and always introducing me as your mentor has not just been encouraging but humbling as well. Thank you for believing in me my brother, it motivated me to go all the way. Special thanks, further goes to Francine Mashabela and Jacob Khunwana for helping with editing. Putting aside time in the midst of other commitments, to edit this book is not easy. Your contribution is acknowledged and appreciated, and may the good Lord bless you.

Last but not least, I would like to acknowledge my sister, Shirley Baloyi for her elegant photographic touch. Your contribution has not gone unnoticed in heaven, my sister. May the good Lord richly bless you.

Author's Quote:

"A decision to engage in love sets you on
a path that determines whether you will
experience heaven or hell on earth"

PROLOGUE

"Did God really say, 'You must not eat from any tree in the garden'? We all know what followed the woman's answer. "You will not certainly die!". More like a guarantee of a better life, the latter words from the serpent seemed enough to convince Eve otherwise, even against the Creator of the very knowledge contained in that tree. She saw that the fruit was good for food and pleasing to the eye, and also desirable for gaining wisdom. She took some and ate it (Gen 3:1b, 4a, 6 NIV). Not only did she eat on her own, but gave some to her husband who was with her, as if to say 'I am not going down alone'.

It is quite disturbing that the human race is falling for the same old trick over and over again – deception by the old serpent called the devil and satan. All he has to do is to cast doubt about what God has said or question the integrity of what He has commanded us to do. A growing number of fatherless family units are confronting us on a daily basis. God is still calling, 'Adam (fathers), where are you?'-they are in hiding from the One who sees everywhere because they have suddenly realised that they are naked. Their way, which appeared to be perfect, has proven to be full of flaws and now they have to run for dear life to hide their nakedness.

If one were to record all the cases we come across in practice during the cause of family therapy, the world would not be able to contain the books written. The miseries experienced by married, divorced and dumped individuals, as well as children resulting from such relationships are beyond description. The family unit is the building block of the church, which is the reason the devil is all out to destroy this in order to render the church ineffective. We see the number of single parents grow by the day, by default or by choice because some individuals are growing sceptical towards the marriage institution. The family unit as designed by God has been distorted.

Mr Baloyi's book comes at a time when there is dire need to go back to the drawing board, and see where we went wrong as an end time church. All is not lost. We have a remnant in the likes of this author who still believes in the sanctity of marriage, whose author is the Almighty. There is a need to re-establish the ancient landmarks as commanded by the Word (Prov 22:28 and 23:10).

The present mess we find ourselves in is as a result of the lie from the pit of hell that we can modify the Word of God to suite our evil desires. These lies range from, 'premarital sex is not so bad as long as we have promised each other marriage', to 'Let's move in together to see if we are compatible partners'. More often than not these plans blow up in our faces and cause such terrible misery that defies any description. Many young couples realise too late that God's Way is the BEST WAY.

This book is recommended to all young people long before they even think of dating, young adults about to get married and even those who have made mistakes and want to repent and do it the Lord's Way. It is also recommended for parents who wish to instruct their offspring in Godly counsel. Finally, 'Blessed is the man who walks not in the counsel of the ungodly, but his delight is in the law of the Lord' Psalm 1:1a, 2b.

I am fully persuaded that many lives will be transformed as they read this great book.

Dr R S Koka (Specialist Psychiatrist).

CONFIGURATION

Dating continues to be at the heart of young people's debates in the church today. This is not surprising, neither should it be something to be frowned at. It is natural for people when they reach a certain stage in life to begin to respond to what their body and mind feeds them in terms of intimately relating to someone of an opposite sex. It is absolutely normal for every young person to feel like and think about dating at some stage. For some, this may come earlier whilst for others a little later.

Naturally, as humans develop physically, sexually, emotionally and spiritually, they get to a point where a desire for someone of an opposite sex becomes inevitable. This desire can be destructive should it fail to be managed properly. Desiring or feeling like getting intimate with someone of an opposite sex, does not necessarily mean it's dating time. In essence, although this is normal, it does not mean that you should always at any given time give in to what your body and mind tells you. Unfortunately, of all the development types highlighted about, the last type, i.e. spiritual development is often never taken into cognisance when a decision to engage in love is taken.

Yes, indeed you've read right; I did say when a decision to engage in love is taken. The latter is one essential aspect of love we will get to learn more about in this book. I pray that the Holy Spirit helps you understand as He reveals to you the real essence of what genuine or true love is. That love, which actually emanates not from the heart, but from the Will. The very love that has God as its foundation.

Another question that has been a thorny issue in the Christian circles is the phrase "waiting upon the Lord". People, particularly youth, are taught and encouraged to wait upon God, who in turn will at the right time provide their suitable life partners. But the question is, how does one practically wait upon the Lord?

We will therefore get to learn in this book what "waiting on the Lord" means and how does one wait upon the Lord. I will further attempt to explain the process of dating in the Christian context starting with how love really unfolds. This is very critical as it defines how and where the relationship will end up. It can also determine whether one will experience a wonderful relationship and marriage or the opposite. The scriptures teach us that as Christians, we should be distinct from the worldly way of doing things. This book is therefore, as the title attests, biased to Godly way of courting as demanded by the holy scriptures.

Although the truth about dating and marriage is found in the bible, as much as it is taught and preached in many sermons given at churches across the world today, it often happens that people would want to sway the scriptures to suite them or come up with justifications for not following and practicing what the Word of God says. The human race perpetually falls prey to the old serpent's deception by believing what God has actually NOT SAID, consequently experiencing hell in their relationships and marriages. Paul in his letter to the Romans encourages us not to conform to the pattern of this world, but for us to be transformed by the renewing of our mind.

> *²And be not conformed to this world: but be ye transformed by the renewing of your mind, that ye may prove what is that good, and acceptable, and perfect, will of God,*
> **Romans 12:2 (KJV).**

What Apostle Paul seeks to teach us through the above scripture is that, there's a particular way of doing things in the Kingdom of God which is totally distinct from the worldly way. In light of the aforesaid, I attempt to zoom deep into what is the Godly way of dating. I also in light of the latter go further and explain the differences between the worldly way of dating versus the Godly way.

A distinction between true or real and simulated or unreal love will therefore be explored in this regard. Later on, the focus will be on how to find a lifetime partner as purposed by God. I also attempt to highlight a very important aspect in terms of how a husband should relate to his wife and vice versa, in order for that marriage relationship that God wills for those He loves, to be realised.

Looking at a very high rate of divorce amongst Christians today, I always get tempted to ask, why? What went wrong? As much as many who divorced and those seeking divorce have their reasons, my question has always remained, if we as Christians, know and believe that God hates divorce, why do we go on and let the courts determine the fate of that which at some point, we believed should not be put asunder, since God is the one who founded it?

Reasons for divorce may be numerous, but I believe we need to focus on the root cause rather than the manifestation of what actually happens in marriage. For me, it all goes back to where it started, which is the basis on which this book is founded, love.

Perhaps it's imperative that we lay a foundation on which this entire collection of the Holy Ghost revelations rest, before delving much into this very enticing subject. The next episode will seek to highlight how the relationship of two spiritually matured children of God is actually a demonstration of how God Himself operate.

CHAPTER 1

The relational nature of God

As images of God, human beings have been designed to operate in relationships. God's plan is for us to first relate with Him, and then with the rest of His creation. He created us to be like Him so that we can relate with Him prior to anything else. People work and function better through relations with each other. It is through this relationship with one another that a true meaning of our existence emerges. We have been created to live and grow in families that make up communities, societies and nations.

This relational nature of humanity starts from that point when God connects a young man and a woman in a process to construct a lifetime relationship from which communities and societies will emerge. Our ancestor, Adam started it all at that point when he exclaimed "This one is bone of my bone, and flesh of my flesh! She will be called 'woman', because she was taken from 'man'" (Genesis 2:23). We all have inherited this relational nature from God Himself. Yahweh, in His powerful and unfathomable nature, when He created us, did that in a relational mode. If you read

Genesis 1:26, you will realise that God was addressing a meeting of some sort.

> *26 Then God said, "Let us make human beings in our image, to be like us". They will reign over the fish of the sea, the birds in the sky, the livestock, all the wild animals on the earth, and the small animals that scurry along the ground.*
> **Genesis 1: 26 (NLT).**

The immediate and obvious discovery coming out of the above verse is that God is talking to some person or persons, which is probably known to you and me as the first person of the Godhead talking to the other two. The above illustration does not at all seek to show that God is divided into many parts nor that there are three separate gods. No! God is one. He is Mighty, Gracious, Loving and Merciful. Genesis 1: 26 above, merely demonstrates one of the divine truths about who God is and how He operates.

We see in the scripture above the first demonstration of a total operation of the Holy Trinity. We see God the Father, God the Son and God the Holy Spirit communing as they plan to create the most special and mysterious being, you. The words "Let us", clearly depict a conversation between persons, which reveals a discussion between three persons of the Godhead as indicated.

One of the deep revelations that I find in the scripture above is that, our God is the God who is relational. Powerful and mighty as He is, God believes in relationships, which is what I believe is one of the reasons He decided to arrange Himself in a Triune order. It is also for this reason amongst others that God created marriage, which He started through Adam in the Garden of Eden. By creating marriage, God was transferring His relational nature in man. It is for this reason that we work and operate in and through relationships. No one can fully function or reach his or her full potential as a loner. When we read the bible from Genesis to Revelations, we find that God, in one way or the other, reveals Himself in a relational manner.

First, God related to Adam by communing with him. When God gave Adam a command not to eat from the tree in the middle of the garden, it was an indication that there has been a direct communication between man and his Creator. That in itself depicts the relationship that existed between God and man since creation. God related with Adam as his Creator and was able to communicate with him anytime and anyhow He desired.

Even after Adam's fall, God continued to relate with him. The fact that God came looking for Adam after he hid himself upon realising his nakedness, was affirmation that even the fall could not nullify God's relation with man, which He further guaranteed by promising man's redemption, Genesis 3: 15. When God said the offspring of the woman shall crush the devil's head, He was actually decreeing the coming of Christ who was to crush satan's head on the cross. The decree eventually manifested when Christ the Redeemer came down to earth to save the world, John 3:16.

By sending His only begotten Son, Jesus Christ, to die for you and me on the cross, God was restoring the relationship between Himself and mankind. Subsequently, we then related back to Him by offering Him our very lives and allowing Him to be King and Master over us, totally controlling the way we lead our lives. As He loved us first, we also love Him, demonstrated in the manner in which we love our fellows.

[19]*We love because he first loved us,* **1 John 4:19 (NIV).**

The above highlight of being loved by God and us loving others through which we demonstrate our love for God, is not really the focus of this book, but a simple demonstration of how God has created us to operate in a relational manner. The focus throughout this book will be on love relationships geared towards marriage that displays the God of love and order.

CHAPTER 2

Engaging in love

*⁷I charge you, O ye daughters of Jerusalem, by
the roes, and by the hinds of the field, that ye stir
not up, nor awake my love, till he please.*
Songs of Solomon 2: 7 (KJV).

It is critical, fellows, that I begin this episode by asking
a question; what does the phrase 'falling in love' mean?
I'm not an English first language speaker, but I believe the
phrase more connotes an expression of the extent to which
one gets attracted to someone than a true meaning of what
engaging in a love relationship entails. If one listens to love
songs many of us love, the emphasis is more on attraction,
feelings and intimacy than anything else.

Most of the time, the extent to which one loves someone
is more connoted by the nature and magnitude of the
feelings one has towards the one allegedly being loved.
Allow me therefore fellows, to use the phrase, "engaging in
love" instead of 'falling in love' as commonly used, and this
is a phrase I will be using throughout. A thinking behind
this will become clearer as you read through.

In the above scripture, King Solomon warns against awakening love before it so desires. This does attest therefore that there is indeed a right time to engage in a love relationship. If there is a right time for love, then love must be something that is entered into with a clear conscience. What King Solomon is basically asserting in his songs (2:7) is that, do not open the gates of love prematurely. In essence, love should be engaged in at the right time as purposed by God.

The fact that King Solomon advises us not to awaken love prematurely is itself an indication that engaging in love cannot be a sudden thing as many have been taught and socialised into believing, but a decision and a choice that must be made at the right time. It's probable as you're reading through, that you begin to ask; "but when is the right time?" Well, that is the very reason why you have your hands and eyes on this very book at this particular moment.

I pray that the Holy Ghost opens your heart to the revelations contained in this book not only for your benefit as a single person seeking marriage someday, but as a means to develop and empower you spiritually in the area of relationships and marriage. Even if you are married, the truths and revelations contained in this book can still help you revitalise your love and comprehend some of the things you may have not really understood before as far as love is concerned, despite your experience in relationships and marriage.

In the episodes to follow, we will try to unpack God's philosophy of love, including how to make a distinction between being in love and just driven by emotions, as well as the true meaning of waiting upon the Lord. God's philosophy of love is basically a description of love as defined in the scriptures. Many people get misled into wrong relationships thinking they're in love. This Book therefore is further intended at assisting by explaining measures through which we can know whether we are in love or just in emotional excitement.

In most of the courtships where one party ends up getting hurt, the likelihood is that either of the parties would have only gone as far as the attraction phase or may have never been really looking for something serious. The above indicated phase will be expanded more later in the book where I will try to highlight what I term phases of the Eros love.

I'm conscious, fellows, that what I'm about to reveal on what love really is and is not, may shock and amaze a lot of you who have been socialised and schooled into believing that love has much to do with feelings than anything else. Let me start my analysis on the phrase "*falling in love*" as commonly used. Many of us use this phrase loosely as we understand it in terms of what it expresses on face value, i.e. to *fall – in – love*. What the latter phrase signifies if one looks at it superficially, is that one trips into love.

It is on the basis of the aforesaid that believing love as blind, moves from the premise that falling in love is not a decision, but a 'blink of an eye' occurrence. The argument in terms of the above is that, just as one cannot decide to fall but stumbles before falling, so loving someone cannot be a decision. Unfortunately this is one of the fallacies that society has instilled in us, which has laid precarious foundations for so many relationships and marriages.

We will now in the next discussion look at how various churches, although connected by one important element of our spirituality, Faith, do not really provide a homogeneous or uniform way from courting to marriage, which unfortunately does not help the situation.

CHAPTER 3

Varying church dogmas

As indicated in the beginning of this book, dating continues to be a central point of debate in the church today. Many people, especially youth, have gone astray in their quest for what has always been termed a "lifetime partner". Some identify their aspired partners as "Mr or Mrs Right". Others have even coined terms like "heavenly dating". You enquire from one church to the next, still there's no consensus in terms of what exactly is the right way to courtship and marriage.

The following are glimpses of what one gathers out there from various Christians, particularly young people.

- *One argument goes, "in my church, when I have seen my wife in a vision, I must inform my pastor for him/ her to deliver the words of love on my behalf";*
- *Another exclaims, "No ways! How do you get married to someone you have not interacted with? When you have problems in your marriage, how are you going to sit down and talk to her, if you never proposed her from the first place";*

- *The other goes "I do not believe that it's necessary for me as a child of God to want to know my partner. Since my God is faithful, He will never give me a partner who's not my match";*

- *"You see, the problem with us Christians is that, we don't enquire of the Lord for Him to guide us in our quest to choose partners. We first identify someone and then want to bully God into accepting and blessing what we have already chosen for ourselves", so goes another;*

- *"Of course courtship is allowed in my church, but there are boundaries. For example, we cannot go to the movies being just the two of us, or maybe visit each other at our homes whilst no other person is home". Whenever we are together, there must be a third person with us";*

- *The other would say, "Yes we are allowed to date, but when the sun goes down, we must be apart by then";*

- *"Yes, in our church we do date, but no kissing and fondling".*

These are amongst others, arguments and contentions by many young Christians out there, owing to the varying doctrines that our various churches hold today.

One Sunday afternoon some few years ago, I attended a youth colloquium in one church in my area. Young people were invited to discuss and share their understanding of what dating within the Christian context is. The colloquium was structured such that men of God from several denominations were invited to sit on the panel, with a purpose for them to receive and respond to various questions from young people.

Although the allocated time was very minimal, at least the deliberations went on far enough that it should have assisted all the youth in attendance to have a grasp of what Christian dating is or is not, and for the panelists to have given the youth a Godly way of journeying towards marriage. Perhaps, the poor planning of the seminar is to blame as it seemed to have failed to achieve what it was organised for and thanks to various doctrines brought into that room on the day, which instead seemed to have left most young people more confused than before.

However, since this book is about discovering and embracing your bone or suitable partner, it is imperative that we briefly look at what engaging in love in its essence really means, since that is where it all begins. Unfortunately, people of God around the world have been schooled into believing that love is a sudden feeling that engulfs you without having given a deep thought of what you are engaging yourself into. This is what brought the coining of contentions like "just as one does not decide to fall but stumbles and fall, so is love, hence the phrase *"falling in love"*.

The argument in terms of the aforesaid is that, just as the latter phrase stipulates, a lover becomes suddenly engulfed by affection for the loved one". It does not see love as a deliberate step that one takes but believes it to be a sudden occurrence. Clearly, the above argument basis more on feelings than anything else. Most of us have been taught that love emanates from the heart. I do not honestly believe so. Love stems not from the heart but the will.

Love cannot be something that suddenly overcomes you without you having given serious scrutiny to what you are committing yourself to. It is a process that develops steadily and goes on to take root in the heart. In essence, love cements itself in the heart but does not originate there. It is a conscious decision that one takes based on a variety of factors. I believe love does not necessarily stem from the heart, but gradually builds up from the will and then permanently takes refuge in the heart. The latter analysis confirms therefore that love is not instant but develops.

Since this book is about love relationship between a man and a woman ultimately planning to get married, the focus will be on the Eros type of love. I personally believe that this category of love also emanates from God. My emphasis and deliberation will therefore be on love as defined in the bible. God's philosophy of love is discussed in the next chapter and provides a basis upon which the discussion throughout this entire book will be based.

CHAPTER 4

God's philosophy of love

Before going into details of how can we discover and embrace our lifetime partners, let us first explore this important component of our lives, love in the broadest sense. Understanding true love derives from comprehending God's philosophy of love. I draw my definition of love from the source of love, God Himself. God has given us a divine understanding of what love really is, 1 John 4:16b. The bible defines love as being patient, kind, not self-seeking, trusting, always hoping, always persevering and never failing (a few selection), 1 Corinthians 13: 4-8.

What I deem most significant from the above is the latter part of the definition, which tells us that *love never fails*. If God is love, and His love endures forever (Psalm 107: 1), then it should be practically impossible for love to cease at some point. This love, which God demonstrated to us by offering us His only begotten Son to die on our behalf, is the very same attitude of love God also intended us to display. Not only in the manner in which we treat our fellow brothers and sisters in our day to day lives, but in our relationships and marriages as well. According to the bible, we are God's friends and Jesus died for us because we are His friends. By dying for His friends, Jesus was therefore demonstrating much greater love, which cannot be compared.

> [13]*Greater love has no one than this: to lay down one's life for one's friends.* [14]*You are my friends if you do what I command.* [15]*I no longer call you servants, because a servant does not know his master's business. Instead, I have called you friends, for everything that I learned from my Father, I have made known to you,* **John 15:13-15 (NIV).**

Lovers must above all else be friends, which is the basis on which successful relationships are build. Friendship is a lifelong process, which is never determined by circumstances, but dictates to circumstances. Fellows, friendship never derives from a one day interaction, wherein two people who just met, suddenly out of immediate excitement of having crossed each's other paths, declare themselves friends for life. It is a process that builds up from a continuous interaction where the earned loyalty, faithfulness and trust of the one party steadily entrenches itself, triggering same from the other.

As the American Poet and Writer, Ella Wheeler Wilcox puts it, "love that has no friendship for its base is like a mansion built upon the sand". Friendship is the foundation of every love relationship, wherein lovers are friends before they are lovers. This is the essence of every love relationship (a mansion built upon the rock).

Indeed, love is a decision and a choice, and the source of love Himself testifies to this. Let's look at the subsequent verse of the above scriptural quotation to corroborate this point. Jesus indicates in verse 16 that He chose to love us.

> *16 You did not choose me, but I chose you and appointed you so that you might go and bear fruit – fruit that will last – and so that whatever you ask in my name the Father will give you. 17 This is my command: love each other,*
> **John 15:16-17 (NIV).**

Jesus chose to love us. In other words, He could have chosen not to since we did not deserve His love, but He took a conscious decision to love us to an extent that He went further and died for us. Why? Because, He considered us His friends. Two people in love, should complement each other. There shouldn't be in anyway two forces pulling to the opposite extremes in a love relationship. According to Antoine de Saint-Exupery, love does not actually consist in gazing at each other, but looking together in the same direction.

My interpretation of the above is that, two people in love complement one another. Although they may be coming from different backgrounds with different interests and personalities, through their love for each other, they find common ground to enable them to journey together. This does not imply that they have the same characteristics or must always agree in everything. However, they do agree probably in the most part of their relationship. Even where they don't, they always find a way to move forward, an element that requires some level of compromise.

As Apostle Paul highlights in one of his depictions of love in 1 Corinthians 13, love is never self-seeking, meaning it is not centred on self but more focused on the other party or the loved one. What this signifies is that love, loves even if it is not loved back. It loves even if the loved one is not so perfect. Real love in this sense focuses on the best interest of the other.

If the world could understand the above aspect, all these atrocious situations we mostly witness once a person loses a lover to someone or for some other reason, would be eradicated. What do I mean? Well, should I lose my loved one to someone or for some reasons, I would not lament my loss in terms of what I may have invested, because my love for her was not dependent on her loving me back or staying with me.

It does not matter how much I may have spent or invested in her but true love is the one that says, "I will always love her." Whatever I would have done for her would not have been influenced by an expectation on my part for her to love or stay with me. It means if my loved one has decided to leave me, I will not resent her. I will not call her names or go all the way out to discredit her.

There can never be "whatever we had, we had" in love, like some of the world's renown artists once proclaimed. Love always has. It never fails nor ceases. Once the choice is made, love sticks through and through. Jesus stuck by you until the point of death. Oh, what a significant "till death do us part" display! I believe this is the very same love attitude our Lord transferred in us for us to display in our relationships and marriages.

Throughout my life, I have witnessed situations where someone who has lost a lover would commit the most atrocious of acts in the name of love. Over and above the news reports we hear, see and read about in the media every day, I grew up witnessing those who should be given love, being battered and abused by those who claim to or at least believe they love them. Men have and continue to commit shameful an inhumane acts, all in the name of love.

One day some years ago in Madidi village where I grew up, I was on my way from Ntolo High School on a cloudy day, when I came across a very disturbing scene. As I walked down the river called Marepe on my way home, my eyes took me east, to the rocky part of the non-perennial river. I was beginning to walk faster as the stratocumulus clouds had just began to let off some drizzly drops. As if I had not just been hastened by the looming down pours, an atrocious view complemented by some horrifying screams, immediately stopped me on my tracks.

I stopped and looked, before taking the next step. Suddenly, I noticed that the screams were coming from a group of school girls crying over one of their sisters who was being assaulted by her boyfriend. With an attitude that appeared like I was capable of rescuing the poor lady, who was way older than me by the way, I immediately ran to the scene. Like those crying poor girls, I upon my arrival stood helpless as this heartless man who was supposed to be the one protecting her lover, unleashed all his martial arts skills on his "loved one."

Albeit the poor lady was finally rescued by one of the girl's brothers staying nearby who was called in to help, the poor lady was left bruised, bleeding and unable to walk by herself. I still remember some of the insults this guy was hurling at her. As we stood there, we heard how the man had bought her jewelry and expensive stuff, as he tore the designer clothes on her and smashing all the beautiful watches, necklaces and rings that he had bought her against the rocks on the side of the river. He repeatedly shouted, "if I cannot have you, no one should!".

This is the man who by his own definition was in love but frustrated by not being able to be loved back or rather "not being loved anymore". As I have indicated above, true love continues to love even if it is not loved anymore. Although I do not know what had happened in the relationship I related above, that is not how genuine love would have reacted. Fellows, that cannot be love but something else far from it.

Please take note that the above analysis seeks to highlight a scenario of a lover who may supposedly "not be loved or loving anymore". Given a plethora of reasons one comes across when interacting with those who have lost or left their lovers in a day to day life, one may assume that, there could have been cheating on the part of the lady or at least suspicion by the gentleman. Perhaps if the lady was cheating, the gentlemen may have started it by cheating first. It could also be that the gentleman or lady may have failed in one of the areas in the relationship to satisfy or meet each other's needs. He could have been too jealous and over possessive such that he came to the wrong conclusion.

Of course, reasons for the above incident could be many and varied, the real reasons which only the two of them will know. However, none and not even the most valid of the reasons would have justified the gentleman's actions.

Now, I want you to think of the above this way. What if the two lovers had displayed the same attitude of love explained above? That love that seek not of its own, but of the other. That love that always protects and never keep record of wrongs. There's absolutely no way that she would have left him and he wouldn't have reacted in the manner he did after being dumped.

In essence, neither the gentleman or the lady would have arrived at a point where "one does not love another any longer" because as the gentleman would be unconditionally giving and displaying his love to his lover, that would automatically trigger and strengthen her love for him as well. In a nutshell, my partner's love and respect for me is enhanced simply because I demonstrated my love to her first. See 1 John 4: 19.

¹⁹We love because he first loved us, **1 John 4:19 (NIV).**

What am I implying by all these fellows? Well, simply that, there's nothing like, one does not love another anymore. Real love just cannot arrive at that point. You simply cannot have loved before but always love. Love that does not always love, is not love at all. You either love or you don't. I know you are probably battling in your mind and thinking to yourself, 'but people always break up or divorce their partners because they don't love them anymore'. True, and yes they do. At least that's the reason they give. But I can tell you for sure that, either those never loved from the first place or were faced with a situation where coming out of that relationship was the only way of saving themselves.

Someone staying in an abusive relationship or with an adulterous partner for instance, cannot in the name of love subject themselves to the horror brought about by such a relationship or marriage. Clearly in such instances, it would be justifiable to quit, however it would not necessarily mean you never loved your partner. Even the Lord Jesus Himself gave that one condition by which one can divorce, that is, marital unfaithfulness. Not that divorce is justifiable, but there are instances where, although not willed by God, it's conditionally permissible.

Let me make this clear; God hates divorce! Under no circumstances would He jubilate upon a crumbling marriage (Malachi 2: 16). I wish to highlight that even though Jesus indicates unfaithfulness as the only acceptable reason for divorce, it can never be condoned or celebrated by God's standards. It has not and will never be God's plan and purpose for a man and a woman to divorce.

> *[4]"Haven't you read the scriptures?" Jesus replied. "They record that from the beginning 'God made them male and female. [5]And he said, 'This explains why a man leaves his father and mother and is joined to his wife, and the two are united into one.' [6]Since they are no longer two but one, let no one split apart what God has joined together.",*
> **Matthew 19: 4-6 (NLT).**

Let's explore the following case scenario. Getty finds herself in an abusive relationship with someone she dearly loves. Despite her hoping for the relationship to change for the better, all that comes her way is a worsening situation. She does not only suffer physical mistreatment but she is emotionally abused as well. She cries for the better part of her relationship and is always in and out of hospital and counselling due to the trauma and pain the relationship brings her. She loves her partner but despite her love for him, she is ultimately forced into divorce. All else she has tried failed, and she now recognises that her continued stay in this relationship will eventually take her very life.

Although Getty loves her partner, she eventually surrenders the marriage she was so expecting to give a lot in. She witnesses her dream of her beautiful son and two daughters growing in a warm, joyous and God fearing family with a loving mother and father, disappearing into thin air. Now, one may ask, if love really endures forever, why did Getty's marriage end in divorce? Does it mean she never loved her partner? Well, not really. As indicated earlier, Jesus Himself gave a condition for divorce.

> *⁹And I tell you this, whoever divorces his wife*
> *and marries someone else commits adultery –*
> <u>*unless his wife has been unfaithful,*</u>
> **Matthew "19: 9 (NLT).**

As I have indicated, God hates divorce as Malachi explicitly expresses. Although Jesus points out unfaithfulness as justification for divorce in the above scripture, in the preceding verse He tells the Pharisees that the only reason Moses permitted them to divorce was because of their stubbornness, because God created marriage for His glory and not to be defiled and tempered with.

> *⁸Jesus replied, Moses permitted divorce only*
> *as a concession to your hard hearts, but it was*
> *not what God had originally intended,*
> **Matthew 19: 8 (NLT).**

It is clear from the above scripture that it was not even God who permitted divorce but Moses. Because the Israelites were very stubborn, Moses had to come up with a civil way by which men could divorce their wives than have these poor women subjected to neglect and emotional torture simply because they have fallen out of favour with their husbands.

God does not approve of divorce unless there's unfaithfulness, which puts the cheated or abused partner at all manner of risks and dangers. This is a very big topic on its own and I will be unpacking more on the subject in my follow up writings.

I believe God would not be pleased with the manner in which Getty's marriage ended. However, God does not want His children to be in bondage nor keep up with hell in their marriages just because He does not approve of divorce. Getty did not file for divorce because she did not love her partner any longer, but did so for her own well-being and safety. She therefore cannot be accused of not having had or demonstrated true love. Indeed, people get separated and divorce every day, with reasons ranging from, "I do not love her anymore", "things are simply not working", "he's not the man I thought he was" etc.

But didn't I say true love lasts forever and never ceases? Can true love arrive at that point of a ninety degrees turn, where the one I used to love before suddenly becomes someone I despise and would want to go all out to inflict pain on, in the name of making her pay for what she did to me? I do not think so. I have already indicated that I draw my definition of love from the source of love Himself, God, and His love indeed never ends as I have alluded but endures forever.

I can confidently assert, fellows that, most of the relationships and marriages that break on the basis of love having ceased, were never based on true but simulated love. The point I'm trying to highlight here is that, real love does not end but lasts forever. In essence, there's simply nothing like 'love does not love anymore'. These are just lies and simulations from the pit of hell.

I would, however, like to highlight the following. The love explained above, is not the kind of love that loves unconsciously but the one that loves unconditionally. God, despite us having rebelled from Him, did not desert us but continued loving us, confirming His love that endures forever. It is from this kind of love where I draw my definition of what true love is and means. Love is not self-seeking but always concerned with the affairs of the other.

God was mainly concerned with my affairs than His, when He sent Jesus Christ to die for me. He was never concerned about how our rebelliousness and dirt would defile His holiness or reflect on His position as God. He was never concerned about His glory, splendor and power when he descended to rescue me and you, but our safe return home. Despite the world not having received Him, God continued to demonstrate His love by giving those who would repent and believe in Him, the right to be called children of God, John 1: 11-12.

The above exploration of the essence of love drawn from God's philosophy of love was just a demonstration of what true love is. Probably by now, the above discussion may have answered a plethora of questions. However, you could probably, still be thinking to yourself, this is so complex and not easy to comprehend. You may be thinking this way since you yourself have been a victim of the so called "*love that ceased*" or yourself are a perpetrator of "*terminated love*". I am confident, brothers and sisters, that the truth the Holy Ghost is about to reveal to us will clear the confusion we may have had or are finding ourselves in.

Fellows, it is very important that we understand feelings as not love but an important part of love, which will be explored in much more detail in the next episode. It's probable now that you are wondering, how then, would you know you are in love. A distinction between true and simulation love is highlighted next to help you to know and determine whether you are really in love or just in emotional excitement.

CHAPTER 5

How do I know I'm in love?

That butterfly feeling in your belly the moment you see that beautiful lady or handsome guy is surely amazing. But engaging in love, would mean you will stick with that person even when times are no longer so amazing. To understand more, please read on the distinction made below between true and simulated love and discover how to differentiate between the two.

I know most people, particularly the youth, have this question rolling on their minds over and over again. I often hear young ladies converse; "how will I know I love him or whether he loves me?" I specifically single out young ladies, not because young men do not go through this challenge but simply because I have been predominantly asked this question by young ladies, most of whom have been hurt in former relationships. They perpetually go around searching for love but only to encounter heartaches and disappointments.

The following distinction between **True love** and **Simulated love** is therefore worth exploring in this regard. Perhaps it would assist to define the terms before presenting the distinction between them. **True love** is love that is real and sincere as professed by the scriptures (see definition in the preceding chapter). True love as the term attests, is real or original love. That kind of love that has God as its foundation. This is love not informed by anything else but the lover or the loving one him/herself.

On the other hand, **simulated love** as the term affirms, is not real or original but counterfeit. I believe this is the kind of '*love*' orchestrated by the devil since it's not original but faked. This love is very much present centred. It's largely a matter of physical attraction than friendship and companionship. Since this love is not real it's much more susceptible to emotional highs and lows. Next, is a distinction between true and simulated love.

TRUE LOVE ⟸ ⟹ SIMULATED LOVE	
✤ True love is that kind of love that develops slowly and then grows gradually with time (refutes notion of love at first sight).	✤ On the other hand, simulated love springs up quickly into bloom but then radically varies in intensity.
✤ When you truly love someone, you always feel secured. You are warm with a sense of your loved one's nearness, even when that person may be far from you at that particular time.	✤ Accompanied by a sense of uncertainty. You are filled with feverish excitement. When the loved one is away, you are so miserable. You can't wait until you see your companion.
✤ This type of love is not self-seeking but other-centered (1 Corinthians 13), meaning it always concerns itself with the welfare of the loved one. Your focus is mostly to ensure that your partner is happy. You always support your companion in good and difficult times.	✤ Longs for more and more self-satisfaction and pleasure. Your focus is more on how the relationship reflects on yourself and your status in society. A typical example of this would be a man who seeks an educated woman simply because he feels she will complement and enhance his already high status in society.

🌿 Although you desire to get married immediately, you know that you can wait. You are certain of one another and can plan your future with complete confidence.

🌿 You want instant marriage because you fear losing your loved one to someone or for some reasons. You are so insecure and feel like delaying may bring your relationship to an end.

🌿 Although physical attraction is a natural and spontaneous part of true love, it's only a component. With true love, you enjoy a sweet comradeship without sharing physical intimacies, i.e. sex, fondling and kissing. You are above all else friends and companions.

🌿 Simulated love is largely a matter of sexual attraction. It's normally difficult for you to enjoy each other's friendship without an expression of intimacy or passion. This is where you mostly hear men demanding sex as proof of love.

🌿 You are always willing to hear the other side. You are willing to give, take as well as compromise. This type of love is rational and stable.

🌿 With this type of love, couples usually find it easy to disagree. The relationship alternates between periods of conflict and of great emotional or physical excitement.

🌿 Reflects trust and confidence. You understand that your loved one will wish to occasionally associate with others (friends, relatives and colleagues). You understand that constant monopolising of each other will eventually choke the relationship

🌿 Habitually brings with it an inability to trust the other person. When the loved one is away, you wonder whether he/she is with someone else. You are jealous when your companion speaks or laughs with someone of an opposite sex. You are too possessive and want your partner all to yourself despite her/him having other loved ones around him (family, friends etc.).

🌿 True love is spacious. Because of it, you wish to grow and become a better person in life. It reinforces standards. You understand that there's more to life than just the love between the two of you.

🌿 Leads you to compromise standards. Your love is not growing influence. It produces sorrow and possible tragedy. All you care about is the excitement brought about by the relationship, making you to forego other important aspects of life.

✤ True love is visionary and focuses not only on today but the future as well. With this love, you can sacrifice instant pleasures for long-term happiness. It brings discipline and order in your life.	✤ Present centered and ephemeral. Never thinks of future consequences, therefore not lasting a lifetime. It mainly concerns itself with the short-lived pleasures brought about by the relationship. Sex and other instant pleasures are at the centre of this relationship. It more lives in the now than the future.

The above analysis clearly reflects love as a process that builds up steadily. This refutes the notion of love at first sight. As stipulated in 1 Corinthians 13: 4-8, love is not self-seeking. Simply put, it never seeks of its own but that of the other. True love allows you the pleasure of leading a healthy and prosperous life. Since you are sure of your love and companion, you are stress free, which allows you to also concentrate on your personal development for the sake of you and your loved one. You want to excel in everything for your beloved just like Jacob.

> [20]*And Jacob served seven years for Rachel; and they seemed unto him but a few days, for the love he had to her,*
> **Genesis 29:20 (KJV).**

With true love, you enjoy your love without physical intimacies. You are willing to forego immediate pleasures for long-term happiness. On the contrary, simulated love is largely a matter of emotions. With this kind, the lover misses a glorious opportunity to choose to love. The "lover" is forced into a relationship by his/her emotions (feelings).

This is the kind of love that I call perverted love and definitely does not have God as its foundation. With simulated love, a person is more in emotional excitement than really in love. You just can't keep your mind off your companion despite other responsibilities you might have. You end up performing very poorly at work or studies simply because your mind is always preoccupied with your loved one.

Fellows, this is not what real love entails. Missing your loved one when she or he is away should not make you miserable. It should be a beautiful feeling that gives you hope and confidence. When two people in love are apart for various reasons, e.g. studies, business or work, missing each other should actually provide some sense of warmness, certainty and security. Because you are certain of your love, you know that your being apart is not a threat to your relationship. You have a sense of nearness to your lover even though she or he is far away.

This does not at all signify that I promote long distance relationships. If I were to give my personal view, I would discourage long distance relationships where possible, particularly for married couples. By my contention above, I seek to show that if you are truly in love with someone, you will have a sense of his/her immediacy, even when that person is far away. Missing your partner does not at all leave you miserable but becomes a beautiful feeling that eases your soul.

As already indicated, love is not a feeling but a decision and a process. Once you begin to get attracted to someone, that's not necessarily love yet, but a mere invitation to be part of this person's life. An attraction begins with a feeling, and feelings are only a part of love. If love were to be predominantly a matter of feelings, it would come and disappear just like feelings. You can never feel the same way all the time. Feelings fluctuate. Today you feel this way, tomorrow the other way.

God created us with emotions for us to experience joy, peace, pleasure and most of all, love. Contained in the emotions is the power to feel, which is the critical component of love. Although love is a decision, it must be felt. Love is expressed through actions. However, it is through feelings that love is experienced and enjoyed. The only problem with feelings is that they have variations and mostly respond to things that are temporary. Things that are susceptible to change or rust. It is for this very reason that feelings must not control us but be managed.

What do I mean by 'feelings react to short-lived things'? For instance, you may develop feelings towards someone based on the way they look, i.e. their body structure, the way they walk, smile or even their voice. Some women are charmed by tall guys, those with biceps and a deep voice while others like well-dressed men or the ones occupying a particular status in society.

Likewise, other men are attracted by curvaceous women, slender, short or those with bigger bodies etc. Depending on one's inclination, these are normally some of the things that attract men and women to their potential partners. For instance if you are intrigued by slender women, the likelihood is that those are the type of women you will predominantly develop feelings towards or be attracted to.

Should the above be your main barometer in choosing a life partner, you run the risk of failing to sustain that kind of a relationship. A slender and curvaceous woman may 10 years down the line look completely different from the way she was when the two of you met. A man may similarly loose his muscular body or high status in society. On the other hand, even as that slender beautiful lady may be able to maintain her shape, you may get used to her to a point where she no longer looks attractive, should your feelings not be revitalized. I will discuss this in my follow up writings.

Was your decision to marry your spouse solely based on her looks or his position? Well, you could be in a bigger conundrum than you could notice. It is for this very reason that the feeling component of love needs to be put under control. Fellows, we need not allow ourselves to be driven by feelings. The fact that King Solomon advises us not to open the gates prematurely, attests that we have the ability to restrain our feelings. Your decision to date that lady must not be driven by how you feel, but by what that person really is, her heart. The bible does highlight that a person is defined not by any other thing, but the heart.

> *[18]But the words you speak come from the heart – that's what defiles you. [19]For from the heart come evil thoughts, murder, adultery, all sexual immorality, theft, lying, and slander,*
> **Matthew 15: 18-19 (NLT).**

> *[23]Above all else, guard your heart, for everything you do flows from it,*
> **Proverbs 4: 23 (NIV).**

In essence, it's all in the heart and everything else flows from there. As the NLT translation puts it, "A person's heart determines the course of his life". A decision to engage in love with someone should therefore not be informed by anything else but that person's heart. But is it not only God who knows the heart? Of course it is. In actual fact, He knows yours even more than you know it yourself. But as indicated in the scriptures above, a person's heart informs his conduct.

Interacting with your potential partner should therefore give you an indication of what kind of a person she is, based on how she conducts herself. The way she views and does things should somewhat give you a clue. Does she love people? Is she easily irritable among other people? Please see phases of the eros love in the next episode for a highlight of all the critical phases of love.

What actually informed your decision to get married? Was it that you could not control your hormones and needed someone to appease your sexual appetite? Were you looking for a helper, a woman of noble character? Should the former describe your reason for marriage, then your marriage has been built on sand. Equally, it could also be the reason why you find yourself always cheating or at least tempted to.

With simulated love, you can't keep hands off each other. Constant kissing and fondling are at the center of your relationship. Your love is predominantly driven by sexual intimacies. Sex becomes the measure of your relationship. With true love, you will apply your mind before giving in to those feelings. Should the person you have feelings towards not represent your ideal woman, even merely entertaining those feelings will be a nonstarter. What do I mean by an ideal woman. Well, I am not at all referring to a flawless superwoman, but the one who has been made right by God. The one who fears the Lord and shuns from evil. Yes…a woman of noble character.

Simulated love does not entertain the future. The focus is on momentary excitement presented by the relationship. This type of love also has too much insecurities. You are always wondering what your partner is doing when she/he is away. There's constant monopolising of each other. The relationship is shadowed by the emotional highs and lows, alternating between periods of conflict and of great emotional excitement. Sex is at the centre and the main measure for this kind of love.

If your partner begins to measure your love for him by the manner in which you give him sex, then that relationship is like a mansion built on sand. Indeed, sex is a gift from God but should not to be engaged in prematurely or used as a means to prove or display one's love. It's a precious gift to be enjoyed by two mature happily married people who love each other.

Let me just for a moment endeavour to explain how is love a decision. To do this, let us explore how God fashioned man. When God created man, He created him in spirit and as spirit (Genesis 1:26-27), put him in the body and gave him a soul (Genesis 2:7). Now, we have the soul divided into three elements, the **Mind** (power to think and reason), the **Will** (power to choose and decide) and the **Emotions** (power to feel).

As I indicated earlier, we choose to love, we don't just feel love. A feeling is only a part of love. In our process of choosing or exercising our will power, we are aided by our mental power, the mind. Simply put, our will power is influenced by our mental power. For example, even though we choose to love, you can't choose without thinking. When you engage in love, it's a conscious decision that you take based on a variety of factors.

The above analysis, confirms therefore, as already indicated that, engaging in love is not just a matter of physical attraction. Albeit the latter is a natural and spontaneous part of true love, it's just only a part. Engaging or "falling in love" is a conscious step one takes informed by a multiplicity of factors. It subsequently goes without saying that you cannot engage in love with someone you have never met before or never had a one-on-one interaction with. You cannot meet someone today for the first time and claim to be in love with that person (love at first sight notion).

Yes, I know for sure that there are people who meet over the phone, Internet etc. and eventually get married. But if you can trace most of such cases, you would realise that, their love most probably begins to build upon their meeting. Their meeting becomes the main catalyst that kick-starts their relationship from which their love starts to develop and grow. It is important, however, for God to not only be at the centre of this meeting but in all the processes preceding this stage. It is important to make God an important part of the equation way before you start with the love journey.

> [3]*Commit your actions to the Lord, and your plans will succeed,*
> **Proverbs 16: 3 (NLT).**

King Solomon advises in the above scripture that we need to involve God in all that we do, so that He can direct us in the way we should take. We need to seek God in everything, including when we enter into the love expedition. Not just at the point where you identify that beautiful lady. It should be a continuous part of your work in the garden as you are busying yourself with all the tasks God has given you, as He had assigned Adam. That way, God will connect you with your partner in the spirit, without you even noticing it. More on working in the garden will be unpacked in one of my publications to come, titled; Staying and Working in the Garden.

God connects people first in spirit, just as He created the spirit man first before forming the dust man. Once you are connected in spirit, it then becomes automatic and easy for you to connect in the flesh. God first connected Adam and Eve in spirit before bringing them together in the flesh. However, for them to connect and relate intimately, there had to be physical attraction. It is just how God made us, which is where the part of emotions (feelings) comes in.

You will notice as you read Genesis 2:22-23 that God did not make Adam notice Eve. It just happened spontaneously. God brought the woman to the man and the man automatically connected with his own flesh and bones. In actual fact, feelings, which are largely a component of simulated love, form a small, yet critical part of true love.

A feeling cannot be love as already highlighted. Feelings can be more like cravings. Perhaps let's explore this practical example for a moment. You could one moment say, "I'm craving coffee". Normally, you cannot crave coffee all the time. This time you have cravings, the next you don't, just like feelings. So if love was a feeling, it would most probably be like cravings. Today you crave, tomorrow you don't. In that case, love would justifiably just come and go as it pleases.

If love was a feeling, which comes and goes, it really wouldn't have its origin from God because the love of God does not come and go but is eternal. It endures forever. As I have already indicated, I draw my definition of true love from the God of love and who is Himself love, which never ceases.

> [8]*He that loveth not knoweth not God; for God is love,*
> ***1 John 4: 8 (KJV).***
> [1]*"Give thanks to the LORD, because he is good; his love is eternal!",*
> ***Psalm 107:1 (GNT).***

CHAPTER 6

Phases of the Eros love

As I have already indicated, if there's a right time to love, it means there's also a wrong time. In other words it is possible that love can be engaged at the wrong time. Something King Solomon sternly cautions us against. If Solomon advises that love should be aroused only when the time is right, then "engaging in love" should be a decision. As a conscious decision that one takes, love then becomes a process. In this episode, I attempt to highlight various phases of love. I have identified five phases that one should go through in the journey of love, to highlight how this important aspect of our lives needs to be approached.

The phases highlighted below are not necessarily a prescription, but a guideline in terms of how the process of true love unfolds. This process would not be possible in the case of that type of love which is predominated by feelings, since that kind, disregards the will power. The love phases below are those consciously gone through with an intention to construct a lifelong love relationship and marriage. The phases are as follows;

- The preliminary phase.
- The charm or appeal phase which has two forms or levels i.e. *the emotive* charm and *personal charm.*
- The manifestation phase.
- The test and endurance phase, and
- The maturity phase.

Kindly take note, fellows, that as it is the purpose and focus of this book, in explaining all these processes, I attempt to also explain how to choose a partner as purposed by God. As much as God provides a lifetime partner, I have also indicated that love is a choice, wherein you choose to get into a relationship or engage in love with someone.

Yes! you do have a choice, even if God is the one who provides. "Can God provide more than one partner?" You could now be asking yourself. Well, not really! However, it is imperative my friend to also take into cognisance that, the ancient serpent, called satan, who leads the whole world astray, is right here with us on this puny blue planet called earth.

> ⁹*And the great dragon was cast out, that old serpent, called the Devil, and Satan, which deceiveth the whole world: he was cast out in to earth, and his angels were cast out with him,*
> **Revelations 12:9 (KJV).**

In the above scripture, John writes about war that broke out in heaven wherein satan and his demons fought against Michael the angel of God and angels under his command. What I mainly seek to highlight in this scripture is the phrase "*and Satan, which deceiveth the whole world*". Satan is not only a liar, killer and destroyer but a **deceiver** as well.

From the day he deceived Eve in the Garden of Eden to date; satan has been in the business of countering the plan, purpose and will of God in our lives. He, irrespective of his hands down defeat in Calvary, continues to work tirelessly up to this day in an attempt to make us do just the opposite of what God has purposed us to do.

> *[17]And the dragon was angry at the woman and declared war against the rest of her children – all who keep God's commandments and maintain their testimony for Jesus,*
> **Revelations 12:17 (NLT).**

After seeing that he had failed to kill the woman by drowning her in the flood that gushed out of his mouth, the devil got enraged and went on to declare war against the woman's offspring. In essence, having been defeated on the cross, satan went on to declare war against the remnants of Jesus Christ of Nazareth, that is those Jesus came to save and left behind when He went back to heaven.

What "declaring war against the rest of her children" implies is that, satan went off against all those Jesus had died for, you and me. Yes he had lost, but went for us who continue to keep the testimony of Jesus. The main part of his strategy is to deceive and confuse us so that he can thwart and veer us from the way of truth and the plan of God. Therefore, part of his plan is to lead us into wrong relationships knowing that we will end up miserable and ultimately, for those who manage to get married, in divorce. He is the father of deception, that's what best describes him, and his deception can be deadly if undetected.

Although God desires you to have a Godly wife or husband, the devil's plan is for you to get into a wrong relationship. This is exactly where the ability to use your will power to choose what is right before you comes into the picture. The devil also knows God's plans about your life. All he does is to bring something that looks like that which God has promised you. If God has promised you an orange for instance, satan will place a lemon right on your path to the orange.

Although the orange and the lemon look the same on the outside, the lemon is bitter inside as compared to the orange. As much as it is God's Will that you experience and everlasting sweetness in your marriage, satan on the other hand is hell-bent to cut your marriage short or make it a bitter experience. If you manage to get married by God's grace, satan will try to make sure you have a bitter marriage for the rest of your life. Therefore, as much as you have the will power to choose, don't just choose anyhow, but choose right.

> [15] *"Now listen! Today I am giving you a choice between life and death, between prosperity and disaster".*
> [19] *Today I have given you the choice between life and death, between blessings and curses. Now I call on heaven and earth to witness the choice you make. Oh, that you would choose life, so that you and your descendants might live!* [20] *You can make this choice by loving the Lord your God, obeying him, and committing yourself firmly to him. This is the key to your life. And if you love and obey the LORD, you will live long in the land the Lord swore to give your ancestors Abraham, Isaac, and Jacob",*
> **Deuteronomy 30: 15, 19, 20 (NLT).**

I believe it's now clear, fellows, that anything that we get ourselves into in this world has to do with choices. And yes! Even in love. The above scripture also indicates that your choice is the key to your life. This is not an easy task, which if not done properly may end up in misery. I thank God that by His grace, He chose to reveal to us His truths, which are unsearchable through a canal mind, but only by His wisdom given to us by the Holy Ghost.

But why did God subject us to this messy affair? Why doesn't He just put before us only good men and women to choose from? Fellows, our God is a good God. He is the only God that I know who gives His people the willpower to choose to serve Him. He is the only God who puts choices before His children. He is a very gentle God who does not bulldoze His way into our lives despite us being the work of His hands.

Isn't this wonderful? Furthermore, God doesn't just give us choices, but guides us through the right ones. It is only when we use our willpower to rebel against Him that things go wrong, just as it happened with our great grandfather, Adam. For instance, if we continue to read the same book of Deuteronomy 30, verses 16 through 18, God goes on through one of His renown prophets, Moses, to highlight to the Israelites the aftermath of their choices, wherein blessing and multiplication would result from good choices, whilst the wrong choice would only bring destruction to their lives.

[16]For I command you this day to love the LORD your God and to keep his commands, decrees, and regulations by walking in his ways. If you do this, you will live and multiply, and the LORD your God will bless you and the land you are about to enter and occupy. [17]"But if your heart turns away and you refuse to listen, and if you are drawn away to serve and worship other gods, [18]then I warn you now that you will be destroyed. You will not live a long, good life in the land you are crossing the Jordan to occupy,
Deuteronomy 30: 16-18 (NLT)

We will now focus on what the first category in the process of love, the preliminary phase, entails.

The meeting or preliminary phase

The choices we exercise in this phase determine the future and success or failure of the relationship. It also informs the decision to allow the interaction to continue or not, based on the shape this preliminary yet critical interaction takes. This episode further seeks to assist youth and young adults or anyone still waiting for a partner to successfully identify the correct Godly fearing partner which to many of us, may not be so clear cut in the scriptures. I repeat; there's nothing like "love at first sight". The latter saying should actually in my view be rephrased to read, "attraction at first sight". I will expand more on this when we get to discuss the second phase of love.

The preliminary phase of love is the very genesis of it all. People first get introduced to each other and then start to interact. Whether personally, over the phone, online etc., before there can be any meaningful interaction, there must be some determinant to this interaction in one way or the other. You may meet someone at a book store, wedding celebration of a friend or relative (like I met my wife), church conference, library, music concert, internet or be referred to someone by a friend. In essence, there can be no meaningful interaction without an introduction.

The preliminary phase is what determines the continuation or discontinuation of an interaction between two people. Whether two people who have just met, personally or through reference, will have a lasting relationship, rests much on the outcome of this first meeting or introduction.

You may for instance in the first meeting ask relevant questions, which can give you some hints about this person before asking for a person's contact number or invite him or her to a church meeting or conference. That is, of course, if your interest is in a God fearing woman or man, which is what this book is biased to. Please take note that this meeting does not solely refer to meeting personally but it could be over the phone, online or through any other means.

This is a very critical phase as it is at this stage that one can determine whether someone is a Christian or not. Inviting someone to a church conference or event, or simply asking very simple yet critical questions somewhere in the middle of your conversations like, "tell me, what church do you go to?", or asking a question meant to probe the person's spiritual position or convictions such as, "what is your view on tithing, etc.?", can be one way amongst others of helping you understand whether the lady or gentlemen you just met is a God fearing person or not.

The above must be preceded by prayer. Not a prayer just before confronting or meeting the person, but as you are busy "working the garden", it is essential that one prays for a God fearing wife or husband, which I believe the faithful God that I'm serving will heed, just as He heeded mine. There's everything you need in the garden. There's no need to labour or toil. We will learn much about staying and working in the garden in my other follow up publications as I have already indicated.

In the preliminary phase, it is essential that interaction be purely at a brotherly or sisterly level without any hint of interest. Alerting someone that I'm interested the moment I meet or realise my interest in her may as well drive me the wrong way. A probability exists that she could be viewing me in the same light as well, resulting in her acting in a manner she perceives acceptable to me. By instantly showing interest, you may therefore run the risk of entering a relationship prematurely without having satisfied yourself of the basics. By the basics, I am referring to the core criteria to be used in choosing that partner, which is obviously a God fearing woman or man.

Let us look at Isaac's example for a moment to corroborate the above. You may probably be wondering how Isaac's example is relevant since he did not choose Rebekah by himself. Well, even though Isaac's wife was chosen for him by his father's senior servant as per Abraham's instruction, I believe there is still something very significant we can learn from the servant's approach. Before taking a decision that Rebekah was a suitable helper for Isaac, the servant adopted a criteria that would aid him to know whether Rebekah is the suitable helper or not. Let's for a moment explore the below scripture.

> [12] Then he prayed, "Lord, God of my master Abraham, make me successful today, and show kindness to my master Abraham. [13] See, I am standing beside this spring, and the daughters of the townspeople are coming out to draw water. [14] May it be that when I say to a young woman, 'Please let down your jar that I may have a drink,' and she says, 'Drink, and I'll water your camels too'- let her be the one you have chosen for your servant Isaac. By this I will know that you have shown kindness to my master." [15] Before he had finished praying, Rebekah came out with her jar on her shoulder. She was the daughter of Bethuel son of Milkah, who was the wife of Abraham Nahor. [16] The woman was very beautiful, a virgin; no man had ever slept with her. She went down to the spring, filled her jar and came up again.

¹⁷The servant hurried to meet her and said, "Please give me a little water from your jar." ¹⁸"Drink my lord," she said, and quickly lowered the jar to her hands and gave him a drink. ¹⁹After she had given him a drink, she said, "I'll draw water for your camels too, until they have had enough to drink."²⁰So she quickly emptied the jar into the trough, ran back to the well to draw more water, and drew enough for all his camels. ²¹Without saying a word, the man watched her closely to learn whether or not the Lord had made his journey successful,
Genesis 24: 12-21 (NIV).

Abraham's senior servant's encounter with Rebekah denotes the preliminary phase discussed above. We learn from verse 16 that Rebekah was very beautiful, a virgin and no man had ever slept with her. However, the servant never used the beauty of Rebekah as a barometer. Instead, he endeavoured to search her heart. When he asked her for water, he knew that Rebekah's reaction would at least give him an indication of what kind of a heart she has. Is she kind? Is she humble or is she a prideful woman?

Indeed! Rebekah's response signified God's answer to the servant's prayer. If you read through verses 22 to 27, you will notice that the servant's prayer was answered and Abraham's desire granted. To have his son take a wife from his own relatives. It is clear from the above that the process of choosing a wife is not a matter of targeting one particular lady because she is beautiful and attractive. It's more about carefully observing the inner person in this beautiful woman. How you identify and choose your partner is therefore key, hence the importance of this preliminary stage.

The disadvantage of failing to do a proper assessment as indicated above is that the person you just met may not be God fearing at all, yet display herself as such, leading you to build on a wrong premise. This is very critical as it feeds into the second stage, the attraction phase. Allowing the relationship to develop further at this stage without having satisfied yourself that the person is God fearing or not would be dangerous, since once the gates of love are open, it may be very hard to close, Songs of Solomon 2:7 (NIV).

Indeed, it does happen that one gets attracted to someone at first contact, but this is only at the *emotional charm level*, which is another form of the attraction phase. There's no way that you can have a *personal attraction* at the first meeting, as this requires you to know someone in person. Surely, personal attraction cannot derive from an hour's interaction, but an emotional charm can. These two forms of the charm or appeal phase will be explained in detail shortly.

Basically, the preliminary phase marks the stage where your relationship with your potential partner begins and continues in the midst of your work for the Lord. Just like Jacob, although you may have discovered your life partner, at this stage, the focus is not much on yourselves but on serving the Lord in your respective cathedrals, should you not both be serving in the same church. Jacob and Rachel did that at the start of their relationship, which was inspired and activated by their meeting at the well.

> [9]*Jacob was still talking with them when Rachel arrived with her father's flock, for she was a shepherd.* [10]*And because Rachel was his cousin—the daughter of Laban, his mother's brother—and because the sheep and goats belonged to his uncle Laban, Jacob went over to the well and moved the stone from its mouth and watered his uncle's flock.* [11]*Then Jacob kissed Rachel, and he wept aloud.* [12]*He explained to Rachel that he was her cousin on her father's side – the son of her aunt Rebekah. So Rachel quickly ran and told her father, Laban.*

> *¹³As soon as Laban heard that his nephew Jacob had arrived,*
> *he ran out to meet him. He embraced and kissed him and*
> *brought him home. When Jacob had told him his story,*
> *¹⁴Laban exclaimed, "You really are my own flesh and blood!"*
> *After Jacob had stayed with Laban for about a month, ¹⁵Laban*
> *said to him, "You shouldn't work for me without pay just*
> *because we are relatives. Tell me how much your wages should*
> *be". ¹⁶Now Laban had two daughters. The older daughter's*
> *name was Leah, and the younger one was Rachel. ¹⁷There*
> *was no sparkle in Leah's eyes, but Rachel had a beautiful*
> *figure and a lovely face. ¹⁸Since Jacob was in love with*
> *Rachel, he told her father, "I'll work for you for seven years if*
> *you'll give me Rachel, your younger daughter, as my wife",*
> **Genesis 29: 9-18 (NLT).**

It is clear as indicated by the above scripture that Jacob's meeting with Rachel at the well, activated the process of their relationship, which eventually ended in marriage. The interaction at the well signifies the preliminary stage. There's something very significant in the nature of their interaction that I want to bring forth here. In his introduction, Jacob explained to Rachel that he was her cousin on her father's side (verse 12).

Jacob's introduction above, was a very significant one because what he was actually saying to Rachel was, *I'm neither a Canaanite nor from any of the foreign nations the Israelites were barred from marrying or giving themselves to in marriage.* You will also note in the following verse that Rachel upon hearing this, immediately ran to her father to tell him the news, which I believe was out of excitement of having discovered a potential husband.

I did highlight above for instance that, upon meeting a potential partner, one of the introductory ways to interacting with this person could be inviting them to a church conference or event, or simply posing questions like, "what church do you go to, or what is your view on tithing"? Abraham's servant strategy discussed above is one example as well. This way, you are able to determine what kind of a person you have just met or being introduced to.

I believe just as Jacob got attracted to Rachel, she also got attracted to him post their introduction and upon realising that Jacob was one of their own, and their marriage would therefore not be contrary to the Will of God. To me, this is evidenced by when Rachel, excitedly ran to her father, Laban, following Jacob's introduction. The same happened with Rebekah. Upon meeting Abraham's senior servant and all that transpired, she quickly ran to her mother's household to tell them all that had happened. I believe her reaction could have also been out of excitement. The preliminary phase directly leads to the next phase to be discussed, the attraction phase.

The charm or appeal phase

The charm or appeal phase is a stage of attraction, which follows immediately after the first meeting or introduction. This is where interest is detected and subsequently acted upon. Whether one will be interested or not depends much on the preliminary or introductory process. I have made it clear earlier that any form of appeal or attraction is preceded by the preliminary or meeting phase.

It is improbable that you can be attracted to someone you have never met or been introduced to before. In essence, you have to meet or at least be introduced to someone before you can be attracted to that person. As already indicated, I have identified two forms or levels of appeal or charm, i.e. *the emotive* and *personal charm*. The emotive charm is very critical as it requires more management than the personal charm.

The emotive charm can easily deceive since it centers more on emotions and is ephemeral or short-lived. The problem with this form of attraction is that it is mostly false. That butterfly feeling in your belly upon meeting or being introduced to a beautiful lady or handsome gentleman may be misleading. It is more often an infatuation, crush or lust than real love in most instances. With men, this feeling is mostly appeased once you have had sexual intercourse with the person you are seemingly attracted to.

This kind of attraction need to be controlled as it does not necessarily signify real love but just a charm. As indicated in the distinction between true and simulated love in chapter 5, real love forgoes this feeling with faith and believe that, if it's real, it will remain intact between the two of you to be enjoyed later. Strongly feeling that a continued successful interaction rests much on instantly appeasing the feeling, could be a warning flag that this is mere infatuation or lust.

Another form of appeal is more personalised and requires real close and much more sustained interaction. This form of attraction which I term *personal charm,* does not happen at a first glance or meeting. It is the form of attraction from which faithful and lasting relationships rest. The more two people who are attracted to each other continue to relate, the more they get to know each other better, aiding their decision to take a long-life journey together. This phase, more or less overlaps or interrelates with the next phase, which I term, the manifestation phase.

In the personal charm phase, the two spouses to be, are presented with a glorious opportunity to serve the Lord together. This enhances their position to learn each other's roles and calling in the Kingdom as well as their traits. 'Together', in this instance, does not necessarily imply walking together holding hands and going to church. What I mean here is that these two serve the Lord knowing they are there and will always be there waiting for each other. The brother knows that the sister is serving the Lord as he is also doing the same. When the time is right, it will be revealed to both of them.

The relationship could be ongoing within the same church or separate churches but the focus is much on the Lord's service than on each other. As the two continue to commune with one another, they enjoy the beauty of sharing the word of God and encouraging each other. The more the brother shares with the sister how blessed he has been by the powerful move of God during a service for example, the more the sister gets encouragement and confirmation that, "this is indeed the man I have been praying and believing God for all these years" and vice versa.

The Manifestation phase

As the subheading itself purports, this is where some elements of affection begin to manifest. The continued interaction that immediately followed post the preliminary phase, begins to gain momentum. Being now convinced of each other's positions in the Lord, the gates of love are now opening steadily. Dependent on the man's state of readiness, love proposition is now made. I say depending on the man's readiness because although the woman is first introduced to the man by God, it is the man who wakes up to discover and embrace his bone. It was not Eve but Adam who exclaimed "At last! This one is bone from my bone, and flesh from my flesh!".

Eve was brought to Adam by God, she did not bring herself to Adam. However, it is Adam who identified Eve amongst all the animals, not God. In essence, God did not identify or pick Eve for Adam, but Adam discovered her himself, and embraced her. This is a very significant point to comprehend. Eve did not come out of the rest of the animals to Adam, but Adam discovered her out of those animals after God formed her from his bone. He then embraced her. Let me corroborate this. First let's explore the book of beginnings chapter 2 verses 21 through 23;

> [21] *So the LORD God caused the man to fall into a deep sleep. While the man slept, the LORD God took out one of the man's ribs and closed up the opening.* [22] *Then the LORD God made a woman from the rib, and he brought her to the man.* [23] *"At last!" The man exclaimed. "This one is bone of my bone, and flesh of my flesh! She will be called 'woman,' because she was taken from 'man.'",*
> **Genesis 2: 21-23 (NLT).**

By the above contention, I do not at all mean Eve literally came out of the animals. What I'm implying is that, Adam had to make the right choice and chose Eve out of the other animals. The above scripture indicates that after putting man into a deep sleep, God made a woman out of his rib and brought her to the man. Remember, this happened in the Garden of Eden, in the midst of all other animals that have always been there.

As Adam woke up, he immediately recognised and felt Eve as a special being connected to him. He had never felt like that before, despite his daily relations with those lions, dogs, cats, birds, snakes etc. Eve was just the right and suitable partner for him. Note however, that when Eve came to Adam's life, she found him working the garden, which is what the Lord had created him to do. This aspect is expanded further in the next episode to follow; waiting upon the Lord.

Upon being introduced to Eve, Adam started a relationship with her and started a family. It is God's Will that we have God fearing families, so that we can beget Godly offspring, which is exactly why God said to the man he had created, "Be fruitful and increase in number". Remember I indicated earlier that satan is here to counter every plan and purpose of God. It should therefore be of no surprise that he attacked Adam and Eve even before they could give birth to Cain and Abel.

By attacking Adam and Eve before they had children, the devil was trying to corrupt the seed. He was trying to disturb the plan and purpose of God, which is for man to rule and dominate His creation. He knew very well that with the corrupted seed, Adam would breed a generation of rebels, who would defy God.

In the manifestation phase, the lover is ready to pronounce and express the words of love. It all gets laid bare now before the beloved, that she is loved. The lover makes his intentions clear that he wants to start a marriage journey. Upon acceptance of the proposal, preparations get under way. Note, however, that this process is not an end in itself.

The fact that the words of love have been pronounced and that the loved one now knows she is loved, does not mean that the journey has come to an end, but the love process continues. Love is a continuous journey that we travel until we breathe our last, which is what I believe is the reason Paul says we should continue paying this debt, which can never be settled.

[8]Let no debt remain outstanding, except the continuing debt to love one another, for whoever loves others have fulfilled the law, **Romans 13: 8 (NIV).**

Remember brothers and sisters, as I have already indicated that I draw my definition of love from God who is the real love. According to Apostle Paul above, love is a never ending debt that we should probably be paying until our last day in this world. Coincidence? No! When the bride and the groom vow, "till death do us part", it is not just a declaration, but a confirmation of what the Holy Scriptures themselves testify about love.

The test and endurance phase

One day in a matrimonial service some time ago, I together with the multitudes who had attended the wedding, was taken aback by the day's pastor's remarks. With the bride and groom itching in their seats for the pastor to come and get done with the most important part of their celebration - the exchanging of vows, the man of God approached the pulpit. Before he proceeded with the long awaited part, he did something very peculiar.

The man of God, with something looking like a small pouch enclosing a book to read from, posed an unexpected question, which probably sent shivers into the spines of those two love birds and guests of the moment. The man of God turned to the groom and asked; "do you love her?" As if asked a question he did not have an answer to, the groom responded hesitantly; "yebo mfundisi", meaning, "yes pastor". "Are you sure?" the man of God continued. "Yes I am", the groom replied.

The poor groom and the bride were so stunned, understandably so of course. Not only them, but also the rest of the assembly, families and friends who were there, myself included. For a moment, it was like we were about to witness a circus which was to turn what was supposed to be a moment of celebration for the two young couple, their families and friends into an embarrassing show. As the pastor continued, it appeared more as if this man of God was on a mission to embarrass the two.

He then responded to the groom's reply. "May I tell you something my dear brother? Unfortunately you do not love this beautiful lady…yet. You are just attracted to her at this time. Come back after 15 to 20 years and confidently reiterate to these multitudes what you are saying now. Only then, will we be convinced, because love is not complete until it has been tested".

The bride and the groom breathed a sigh of relief. At least, there was nothing untoward the pastor was about to reveal about either of them. All he was doing was teach them what real love is in the context of what they were about to commit themselves to through their exchanging of vows. This real love has less to do with just the feeling they had towards each other, but everything to do with the sustainability of that feeling even at times when things would not be that exciting anymore.

I did learn one thing or two from the above events. Whether charmed by a beautiful lady, emotive or personal, my true love will actually be demonstrated by the way I stick with my partner through trials and troubles. This love is displayed as I continue to support her all the way, in sickness and in lack, in agreements and disagreements, when she does things right and even when she doesn't. It is by my endurance through all these that my real love gets tested and proven true.

I'm not at all implying that you need to focus on proving your love by doing all these things. What I'm saying fellows is, if you love someone truly, you will always love her unconditionally and not only in good times. You will continue to love him even after he loses his job or brings you bad debt. Your love is not conditioned by circumstances or situations. This is the phase of love where the endurance component reflects itself, where love endures even in the midst of trials and troubles.

The maturity phase

This is the stage where everything begins to come together. Passing the test indicated in the *test and endurance phase* above, is an indication that your love is real since it has stood the test of time. This does not at all imply that once you get married, you need to expect unpleasant experiences such as lack, conflict, sickness etc. All it signifies is that although relationships, particularly marriage, cannot be all rosy but rocky at times, when the trouble times strike, love endures.

Love triumphs, conquers and is never disappointed. Love perseveres and is always faithful. Love promises and always sees through what it commits. The above is a simple teaching that true or genuine love, loves unconditionally irrespective of situations and circumstances. Love is not meant to be simply said but acted. When you love someone, you go beyond the expression and demonstrate this love. I'm not talking here about demanded love but the one that is willingly given and received.

At this stage, the lover is at that point where he understands her partner. Under no circumstances am I implying that the lover has come to the point of complete knowledge of his loved one. Knowing a person in totality is a very complicated and a lifetime process. However, relating and communing with a person on a daily basis brings you to a closer and better understanding of that person every day.

In a nutshell, your love has developed and matured to a point where you know how to react to certain situations. For instance, you are now aware that when your partner just nods after you have said something without saying a word, something is bothering her. You know very well that when you hear the call, "Klaas!" Instead of "love", something is not right somewhere, and calls for your attention. Your relationship has now developed or matured to the point where even if she responds by saying, "I'm fine!", to your question, "What's wrong love?", you know she's not telling the truth. Without critiquing her and complaining about her not being honest or trusting you with her feelings, you go, "I understand honey…I understand", as you wrap your hands around her.

You will realise that in the beginning of your relationship, particularly from the appeal phase through to the manifestation phase, most of the issues that make you fight much emanate from you not yet understanding each other. Being entities in your own right, and having completely varying backgrounds and upbringing, it becomes difficult understanding how your partner behaves or does things sometimes.

It is through the manifestation phase where you continue to realise why God has really connected you to your partner. As your relationship grows, you will have more discoveries about her. God will continue to reveal to you why He gave you this partner and how much you need her in your life. The more you know about your partner, the more you love her, not tolerate her. As you grow and mature together, the more you grow closer to each other.

As I get to understand my partner's strength and weaknesses, the more I'm better placed to support and respect her, which entrenches her love for me even further. As she becomes more conscious of the love I have for her, which is demonstrated by my actions (supporting her no matter what weaknesses she has or displays), the more she does the same with me, embracing my weaknesses as well. This then leads to a point of unconscious competition between us, which centers around how the one secretly strives to love and support the other, thus bringing an element of sacrifice from both of us. I will dwell much on this aspect of unconscious competition in one of my follow up publications.

CHAPTER 7

Waiting upon the Lord

Searching through the scriptures, one quickly learns, particularly from the first book in the bible that, God is the one who identifies the need for a partner and provides accordingly. We also learn that when God provides, He does not only provide a helper but the one suitable just for you. In this episode, we will look at what 'waiting upon the Lord' means. We will also learn how to wait for a lifetime partner. How waiting upon the Lord is not inaction but an action in itself. The next discussion also briefly looks at how some of the renowned men of God in the bible, demonstrated the importance of waiting upon the Lord. Let's start with Adam.

Many renowned preachers have preached countless sermons on the importance of waiting upon the Lord. We have in so many respects heard how patience is one of the fruits of the Holy Spirit and therefore a critical attribute to have. But what does it really mean to wait upon the Lord, or rather to wait patiently? Is it a process of waiting to hear the word from God or His prophets every time after vehement prayers? Does one have to wait for some moment in the middle of the night or at daybreak to have a dream or vision?

Normally, when you wait for something or someone, you mostly sit and be on the lookout. You wait in anticipation of that which you are hoping for. If what you are hoping for does not emerge or delays, you may decide to keep hoping and continue waiting or become impatient and stop waiting. Should you elect to wait, at least you are guaranteed that you will get home. It may be an hour, two hours or more, but one thing for sure, you will get home. The bus running behind schedule could be late or broken. Whether it gets fixed or not, at least the next or second next or third next bus, will eventually come.

On the other hand, your impatience can lead to two things; you may totally abandon the waiting or resort to an alternative to ease your impatience. Should you totally abandon the waiting and decide to wander around because you just can't wait for the delaying bus, there's one thing for sure. You will never get home. Secondly, your impatience may lead you to decide to take a taxi because you are in a hurry.

The above option would then mean more costs in taxi fare for you. You had not planned and budgeted for a taxi, but because of your impatience with the bus delaying, you opted for a taxi, meaning more costs for you plus a day's bus fare forfeited if you were using a weekly ticket. In essence, should you elect the alternative, instead of being patient, you must therefore expect an "Ishmael" instead of an "Isaac".

Waiting upon the Lord in this instance is nothing close to the scenario related above. It does not at all mean simply sitting back and doing nothing, fantasising about your dream wife or husband or exploring other alternatives because you feel the Lord is taking time to answer you. As indicated before, waiting upon the Lord is actually an action in itself. It means believing and trusting God for your marriage partner as you are focused on the assignment God has given you.

Let us briefly go back to the period before the fall of man. It's very clear from the book of beginnings that working the ground was one of the reason Adam was created. As clearly indicated in Genesis 2, Adam was amongst others created and put in the Garden of Eden to take care of it and ensure that he keeps it in the condition God wanted it to be in.

> *⁵Now no shrub had yet appeared on the earth and no plant had yet sprung up, for the Lord God had not sent rain on the earth and there was no one to work the ground.*
> *⁸Now the LORD God had planted a garden in the east, in Eden; and there he put the man he had formed.*
> *¹⁵The LORD God took the man and put him in the Garden of Eden to work it and take care of it,*
> **Genesis 2: 5, 8, and 15 (NIV).**

The bible tells us in verse 5 of the above scripture that no shrub of the field had yet appeared on the earth and no plant of the field had yet sprung up, for the Lord God had not sent rain on the earth and there was no man to work the ground. The closing part of verse 5 indicates that *there was no man to work the ground*, attesting that man was indeed created to work the garden. This point is sealed and confirmed by verse 15, which reads, *"The Lord God took the man and put him in the Garden of Eden to work it and take care of it"*.

When God gave us permission and power to dominate and subdue the earth (Genesis 1: 28), He actually intended to dominate and take control of the world Himself, but chose to do that through you. In essence, God wanted us to work with Him in displaying His power, dominion and wisdom to the world. We are therefore supposed to be God's partners in the garden.

> ⁹*For we are fellow workmen (joint promoters, laborers*
> *together) with and for God; you are God's garden and vineyard*
> *and field under cultivation, [you are] God's building,*
> **1 Corinthians 3: 9 (AMP)**

Now, let me try to explain what 'work in the garden' meant. God created Adam and placed him in the Garden of Eden to "work" not "toil". Perhaps before going any further, let us try to unpack these two concepts. According to the dictionary definition, to work means *"activity involving physical or mental effort done in order to achieve a purpose or result"*. On the other hand, toiling is defined as *"working extremely hard or incessantly"*. It is also defined as *exhausting physical labour.*

God put Adam in the Garden of Eden purposely to work it or simply take care of it. Because he was created to take care of the garden, working the garden was enjoyable to him since it was his nature. It was a pleasing and joyous activity that man always looked forward to. It was only after man sinned that this work became a hard and exhausting labour.

In essence, working in the Garden of Eden was something that was gratifying to man since it was part of the purpose of his creation. As God directly communed with him every day, Adam delighted in giving God a good report every time He walked the garden. It was wonderful and enjoyable with no grumbling or complaining about working conditions. Life in the garden was so good and perfect. There was no labouring and sweating. Toiling only came as a result of God's curse due to Adam's disobedience.

> *[17] And to the man he said, "Since you listened to your wife*
> *and ate from the tree whose fruit I commanded you not*
> *to eat, the ground is cursed because of you. All your life*
> *you will struggle to scratch a living from it". [18] It will grow*
> *thorns and thistles for you, though you will eat of its grains.*
> *[19] By the sweat of your brow will you have food to eat until*
> *you return to the ground from which you were made. For*
> *you were made from dust, and to dust you will return."*
> **Genesis 3:17-19 (NLT).**

Just take note of the closing phrase of this verse, *"All your life you will struggle to scratch a living from it"*. Before Adam sinned, he was working the garden as a God given task, which was enjoyable to him without any struggle. "Work" was part of his nature since it was God's purpose for him to take care of the Garden of Eden by working it. It was after he sinned that Adam fell from grace and started toiling and labouring hard for everything. The work that used to be enjoyable and fulfilling to him had now become a painful and exhausting labour.

Adam's waiting upon the Lord for a wife was signified by his work in the garden. He waited upon the Lord through fulfilling his God given role of working the garden. A need for a suitable helper arouse in the course of his business with the Lord. Despite all the pleasure and joy Adam enjoyed as he lived and worked in the Garden of Eden, still there was no suitable helper for him, until God put him into a deep sleep to make him a partner. God was aware that for Adam to effectively dominate and continue to perform well in his assignment of working the garden, he needed a helper. The first operation to have ever been performed in the history of mankind, was performed by the Almighty Himself.

[21] And the Lord God caused a deep sleep to fall
upon Adam, and he slept: and he took one of his
ribs, and closed up the flesh instead thereof,
Genesis 2: 21 (KJV)

As already indicated, in the beginning, God created man and placed him in the garden to take care of it. After God created all kinds of creatures, He brought them to the man to name them. Adam gave every single animal a name and continued to work in the garden as assigned, ensuring that every time God moved around in the garden, He found it clean and in order.

Adam was focused on his Godly given assignment, up to the point where the work became too much for him to do alone. It was at this point where God saw that it was not good for him to be alone and that he needed a helper. In a nutshell, waiting upon the Lord means carrying on with the Lord's work trusting Him for his provision at the right time. Let's explore the following scripture.

[20b] "But for Adam [h] no suitable helper was found. [21] So
the LORD God caused the man to fall into a deep sleep;
and while he was sleeping, he took one of the man's
ribs [i] and closed up the place with flesh. [22] Then the
LORD God made a woman from the rib he had taken
out of the man, and he brought her to the man.
Genesis 2:20c-22 (NIV).

There's a very significant point that I'm gathering from this scripture. As Moses highlights above, God must have explored all of His creation to find a suitable helper for Adam, but to no avail. The fact that no helper was found for Adam attests that there had been an attempted search.

Though all of God's creation was good (Genesis 1:31), still, God could not find a suitable helper for Adam.

How could this be? I believe that God, after an unsuccessful search, went on to realise that the only helper in whom Adam would find joy, happiness and fulfillment would have to come out of Adam himself. This helper would share the same vision with her companion. They would both be able to look together in the same direction. They would above all else be companions.

Adam waited for his lifetime partner, as he was joyously carrying on with his work in the garden. The glory of God was all around him and he very well communed with his Creator. As children of God we should first identify our God given purpose here on earth before we can discover our partners. Upon discovering our purpose we therefore begin to do that which God has purposed us to do.

As long as you remain, and not just remain, but continue to work in the garden, your partner will emerge without you having done any search, just like Adam. My activity in the garden automatically attracts my suitable partner. Waiting upon the Lord in simple terms therefore means, working in the ministry in the area of your gift or calling. You continue with the work the Lord has assigned you and He in turn will give you what you need.

> [31]*So do not start worrying: 'Where will my food come from? Or my drink? Or my clothes?'* [32]*(These things are the things the pagans are always concerned about.) your Father in heaven knows that you need all these things,* **Matthew 6: 31-32 (GNT).**

In essence, it should not be the preoccupation of a child of God to go out searching for a partner. When the time is right, the Lord will open your eyes to enable you to discover and embrace your bone. In actual fact, waiting upon the Lord is an action in itself as I have already indicated. How is it an action? Simply in that, you continuously serve the Lord while you wait for Him to bring someone who will eventually attract you and capture your heart. That's how it also unfolded with Adam.

Ask yourself the following questions; Why was I conceived? What is really my calling? What is my gift in the house of God? Basically, what informs my existence? As children of God, it's essential that we first find answers to the above questions before we can even think of lifetime partners. Once I know why I am here on earth, as well as why I am placed in the local church I'm in, then I won't even have to ponder around the question of finding a partner.

Occupying oneself with the Lord's work automatically attracts your partner and that is exactly how you wait for a partner suitable just for you. For as long as we remain in the garden, work becomes pleasurable, gratifying and enjoyable. It's only when we fall outside the garden that we labour or sweat for things. There's really no sweating and labouring in the Garden of God. In essence, you can't toil for a blessing. When you are blessed, it's something no one can take away from you (see numbers 23:8). We toil and exhaust ourselves once we are outside the garden, which is where the devil is determined to keep us despite God having crafted our way back through Jesus.

Another man of God from whom we can further learn what waiting upon the Lord signifies is Isaac. Just like Adam who met Eve while busy working in the garden, so did Isaac. Let's quickly turn to Genesis 24, verses 62 through 64 to affirm the latter.

> *⁶²And Isaac came from the way of the well Lahai-roi; for he
> dwelt in the south country. ⁶³And Isaac went out to meditate
> in the field at the eventide: and he lifted his eyes, and saw,
> and, behold, the camels were coming. ⁶⁴And Rebekah lifted up
> her eyes, and when she saw Isaac, she lighted off the camel,*
> **Genesis 24: 62-64 (KJV).**

Fellows, I want to draw your attention to the phrase *"And Isaac went out to meditate in the field."* The latter is a very important phrase to understand. What was Isaac meditating about? I believe he was meditating about God. He probably had taken a walk to have a quiet time with the Lord. You will realise when you read the whole chapter that, that very day Isaac went meditating, is exactly the same day he met his wife Rebekah. I believe Isaac had not just gone for a walk but took a stroll with the Lord.

Rebekah, his wife to be, found him in business with God. It is not indicated what Isaac was meditating about, but I believe it was far from talking to God about his need for a partner because that had been predestined without even his knowledge. When you read all the preceding verses of the above scripture from verse 1, you will realise that, Isaac's father Abraham, discussed Isaac's wife secretly with his senior servant. Abraham made his servant swear that once he's gone, he shall never take a wife for his son Isaac, amongst the Canaanites.

Similarly, the story of Jacob also signifies how one waits upon the Lord for a suitable partner. When Rachel came into Jacob's life, she found him busy and focused on his work as he had been assigned to do, just like Adam. In other words, when the right time arrived for God to bring Jacob a suitable helper, He did not find him idle while fantasising about his lifetime partner.

What I need you to take into cognisance here, fellows, is that when Jacob met Rachel he was on a Godly assigned project, Genesis 28: 3-5. You would notice after reading verses 3 through 4 that Jacob was not just on a journey but a blessed one.

> *³May God Almighty bless you and make you fruitful and increase your numbers until you become a community of peoples. ⁴May he give you and your descendants the blessing given to Abraham, so that you may take possession of the land where you now reside as a foreigner, the land God gave to Abraham. ⁵Then Isaac sent Jacob on his way, and he went to Paddan Aram, to Laban son of Bethuel the Aramean, the brother of Rebekah, who was the mother of Jacob and Esau,*
> **Genesis 28: 3-5 (NIV).**
> *²⁰Then Jacob made a vow, saying, "If God will be with me and will watch over me on this journey I am taking and will give me food to eat and clothes to wear ²¹so that I return safely to my father's house, then the LORD [g] will be my God ²²and [h] this stone that I have set up as a pillar will be God's house, and of all that you give me I will give you a tenth."*
> **Genesis 28:20-22 (NIV)**

The above quotation clearly attests that Jacob was on a journey with the Lord. You could ask, how? Well, I guess your question triggers another. Could Jacob ask the Lord to watch him on a journey he never purposed him to take? I believe not. Jacob was very well in the Will of God. He met Rachel while he was busy with the Lord's business, just like Adam. Looking into Jacob and Rachel's relationship, there's one important thing that needs a highlight. The fact that Jacob did not idle for fourteen years waiting upon the Lord, has something significant that all singles in the church need to grasp.

Upon discovering Rachel, Jacob embraced her. His conduct subsequent to meeting Rachel proved he truly loved her. As much as he could have preferred to marry her at once, he knew he could wait. I indicated in the distinction between true and simulated love in chapter five that with true love, you know you can wait, despite your desire to get married immediately. Jacob also displayed this element of true love. Even though he waited seven years for Rachel, the bible records that those years seemed like a few days to him (Genesis 29: 20).

By waiting, I'm not at all implying cohabiting or dating your partner for years before marriage in the name of true love. Waiting in this instance means because your love is genuine, you are willing to forego immediate pleasures for long-term happiness, which brings self-discipline and order in your life. Although instant marriage is desirable, you know that you can wait. You are certain of one another and can plan your future with complete confidence. Marriage is not informed nor hastened by the insecurities of losing your partner.

As the book of Genesis 29 above records, Jacob served Laban for seven years to have Rachel. It's important to note that Jacob never cohabited with Rachel, but waited to have her legitimately, after serving his uncle, Laban. Let's explore the following verse of the same chapter.

> *²¹Then Jacob said to Laban, "Give me my wife. My time is complete, and I want to make love to her.",*
> **Genesis 29:21 (NIV)**

Once he had finished serving Laban, Jacob demanded his wife. He asked his uncle to give him Rachel because he wanted to make love to her. The time was now ripe for him to have his wife as per the agreement he had made with his uncle. He had served seven years for Rachel, without touching or laying with her. There had surely been no sexual relations between Jacob and Rachel during the period when he was serving Laban, which is why he specified when he demanded her that he wanted to make love to her.

As Jacob awaited his future wife, he occupied himself by working for Laban. Upon completion of his service for Laban, he longed for his wife and wanted to be intimate with her as per the last part of the above verse because the time was now ripe. It would have indeed been illegitimate for Jacob to have touched or made love to her before they were legally married.

Cohabitation has not and will never be sanctioned by God. God's purpose is for a male and female to be joined together in holy matrimony before they can be intimate or enjoy whatever right to be exercised by a married couple. Marriage is an institution created by God to reflect His glory. Cohabitation can therefore never be acceptable by God's standards. It is indeed sad that today the world witnesses a countless number of Christians who live together without being married yet see no wrong in that. Many are actually justifying the latter by indicating that they have no funds to get married. All this is done in the name of loving and being faithful to each other.

Some years ago while I was still studying at the University of Pretoria, I boarded a bus with one sister I had known for some time during our school years. Although I had known her long before I met the Lord, that day when we met in the bus we were by the grace of God, both born again. It goes without saying what the heart of our conversation was.

As we were busy sharing about the goodness, love and power of God, there came a moment where she shared about her relationship. She indicated to me how she was in love with her boyfriend who happened to have fathered her little girl. Despite her, in her very own words not desiring the situation as it were, she nonetheless went on to justify it.

In my friend's view, their cohabiting was not wrong nor was it against the Word of God. "We are madly in love, and are faithful to each other! Not by chance have any of us cheated on the other before. We are not promiscuous! Surely that should count for something!", so my friend exclaimed. In her opinion, their love was all that mattered. Their faithfulness to their relationship even counted the more, so she was convinced.

For a moment, it appeared like I was incapable of giving her advice. After all, I was single, with no girlfriend at the time. I was also just only a year in salvation, meaning she was my senior in the Lord. At least that's what I thought myself. Who was I, therefore, to condemn her for her actions and for defending what she believed God Himself sanctioned.

Despite my conscience having the better of me, inferiority got the best. I was just a young, newly converted Christian facing a well-seasoned child of God who probably was more experienced than me. Not only in the things of God, but in love matters as well. If I only knew better at the time, I would not have suppressed the Holy Ghost's counsel and motivation in me at that moment, and would have told her to her face that she was driving full speed on the wrong highway.

Unfortunately, this is the view held by most Christians around the world even today, who would go at great lengths to twist the holy scriptures to suite their situations. I believe it is for this reason that Paul, as much as he would have preferred to advise us to remain single, encouraged us to marry.

> [8]*So I say to those who aren't married and to widows – It's better to stay unmarried, just as I am.* [9]*But if they can't control themselves, they should go ahead and marry. It's better to marry than to burn with lust.*
> **1 Corinthians 7:8-9 (NIV).**

Paul in verse 9 of the above scripture, indicates that if people cannot control themselves, they should go ahead and marry. Paul from the above scripture advises us that, should we not be able to control ourselves, we should marry to avoid burning with lust. This will also save us from engaging in fornication or premarital sex. However, those who choose not to marry should not be castigated simply because they choose not to marry. Actually, Paul argues that they choose right, as long as they are able to control themselves. However, the scenario related above is clearly not representing someone who is able to control herself. The lady continuously engaged in sex with her boyfriend in the name of love, even if they were not married.

Paul in the scripture above, was seeking to deliver a message to the church. Rephrased, I believe this is another way Paul could have put it; *"So I say to you who are not married, it is better to stay unmarried just as I am. But if you cannot control yourselves, and since you know God forbids fornication, it is better for you to marry, than burn with lust, which you may eventually give into".* I believe God hates cohabitation as much as he does divorce and we as His children should equally condemn such practices, especially amongst Christians.

CHAPTER 8

How to find a lifetime partner?

More than often a question is asked in the church, how does one find a suitable lifetime partner? One brother in our church asked me a question just before a gents ministry service some time ago. He wanted to know if I believed that every person in the world has a suitable wife or husband waiting for them somewhere. I do not really know why he asked the question, neither did I attempt to fathom further. Instantly, without even having given thought to what was behind the question, I replied, "yes, I believe so".

I can still remember the famous Yahweh's utterances, which I had read and heard a lot of, triggering my above abrupt response. The words; *"It is not good for the man to be alone. I will make a helper who is just right for him"*, kept on ringing in my ears as I gave that short response. The relived sound of that phrase, as if I was there when God the Father Himself uttered the words, triggered my answer to the brother. The lives of Adam, Isaac and Jacob as discussed in the preceding episode, do confirm that indeed God is the provider of all our needs. If He was able to provide them suitable partners, He will provide you as well.

All men of God referenced in the previous chapter met their partners while occupied with the Lord's business. Adam didn't even have to ask of the Lord, but God Himself recognised his need for a helper. It is God who realised that Adam needed someone to help him with the work in the garden. Adam did not even know that there could be someone outside all those animals who could complement him even better. Actually, all those men of God, Adam, Isaac and Jacob, had their wives predetermined before they could even realise that they needed partners.

God fashioned Eve before Adam could even realise there was one. Isaac's wife was discussed by his father Abraham and his senior servant before Abraham passed on. Jacob, was directed by his father Isaac where exactly to get a wife and what kind of a wife he should choose. God knows very well that you need a companion and he'll direct and provide for you according to His riches. Let's explore the following scripture in this regard. I find in the book of Genesis, confirmation that indeed God is the one who finds a partner for you. All you need to do is discover her or be discovered by him.

> "²⁰So *the man gave names to all the livestock, the birds of the air and all the beasts of the field. But for Adam no suitable helper was found.* ²¹*So the LORD God caused the man to fall into a deep sleep; and while he was sleeping, he took one of the man's ribs and closed up the place with flesh.* ²²*Then the LORD God made a woman from the rib he had taken out of the man, and he brought her to the man.* ²³*The man said, "This is now bone of my bones and flesh of my flesh; she shall be called 'woman, for she was taken out of man."*
> **Genesis 2:20-23 (NIV)**

In the kingdom of God we don't go around searching for Mr or Mrs Right as the world has coined the term, but God, our provider is the one who sees to it that you do not only discover your lifetime partner but the one who will complement you in all respects. In the above scripture, we see God Himself being the one who recognised Adam's need for a helper, not Adam.

Most interesting is that God realised the need and acted even before Adam could realise. Actually, Adam just occupied himself with his Godly assigned work, while God in the meantime searched a partner for him. He continued to focus on the purpose God created him for than worrying himself about what partner will be suitable for him, which is God's responsibility anyway. As we have learned in the preceding episode, waiting upon the Lord is not inaction but an action in itself.

Looking at the story of Jacob, one finds an excellent example of true love, which he displayed by not giving in to his fleshly desires to get intimate with Rachel. Jacob focused on his future with Rachel, while he continued with his work. This brought order and discipline in his life. To show how happy and certain Jacob was about his love for Rachel, even those seven years he worked for her appeared to be like a few days to him.

Jacob was truly in love and not just driven by emotions. He knew that he could wait than be hasty. He was sure of his choice. He did not at all fear losing Rachel as he worked through the entire 14 years waiting for his uncle to release her to him. Another important lesson to take from the story of Jacob is that he did not marry an unbeliever. If you read carefully from Genesis 28 through 29 you'll notice that Jacob kept his father's (Isaac) command not to take a wife from the Canaanites, which is what Isaac also did when he married Rebekah. Apostle Paul also warns us against doing things the worldly way in Romans 12:2.

> *²And be not conformed to this world: but be ye transformed*
> *by the renewing of your mind, that ye may proof what is*
> *that good, and acceptable, and perfect, will of God,*
> **Romans 12:2 (KJV).**

Not being conformed to the world signifies living a life that pleases God, which means shying away from evil or ungodly ways as much as possible. It means the way we do things must be different from the worldly way of doing things in all respects, including the kind of relationships we get ourselves into. Our journey to marriage must be different from the world's way. Jacob basically did not conform to the ways of the world of his era by not taking a wife from the Canaanites as commanded by Isaac his father.

> *¹And Isaac called Jacob, and blessed him, and charged*
> *him, and said unto him, Thou shalt not take a wife of the*
> *daughters of Canaan. ²Arise go to Padan-aram, to the house*
> *of Bethuel thy mother's father, and take thee a wife from*
> *thence of the daughters of Laban thy mother's brother.*
> **Genesis 28: 1-2 (KJV).**

In today's terms, taking a wife from the Canaanites would simply mean giving oneself in marriage as a child of God or a believer to someone who is not. Isaac had a very good reason why he instructed Jacob not to take a wife for himself from the Canaanites despite how rich and beautiful women there were. He understood very well that light and darkness would not mix.

As you read one of the books of Moses, Deuteronomy, you will notice that God did command Israel that, once they have taken over and settled in Canaan the promised land of milk and honey, they should not adopt the lifestyles of inhabitants of that land, not even to take their wives or give their daughters to them in marriage.

> *²And when the lord thy God shall deliver them before thee; thou shalt smite them, and utterly destroy them; thou shalt make no covenant with them, nor shew mercy unto them: ³Neither shalt thou make marriages with them; thy daughter thou shalt not give unto his son, nor his daughter shalt thou take unto thy son. ⁴For they will turn away thy son from following me, that they may serve other gods: so will the anger of the Lord be kindled against you, and destroy thee suddenly.*
> **Deuteronomy 7: 2-4 (KJV).**

The reason why God does not want us to marry or give ourselves in marriage to unbelievers is that, He is saving us the trouble of being burdened by those not sharing the same faith with us. Just imagine this, brothers and sisters; having to convince an unbelieving wife or husband to take ten percent (R10, 000) of a R100, 000 income to the house of God. The above statement may have probably almost knocked even you as a Christian struggling with the tithe principle, off your chair. What more then, for someone not sharing the same faith with you?

It is on the basis of the aforesaid amongst others that God through Moses cautioned the Israelites that should they intermarry with the Canaanites, their sons will be turned away by the Canaanites daughters from following God, driving them to serve other gods. Paul also warns against burdening ourselves with people of foreign beliefs and practices. He highlights this aspect very well in his second letter to the Corinthians.

> *[14]Be ye not equally yoked together with unbelievers: for what fellowship hath righteousness with unrighteousness? And what communion hath light with darkness? [15]And what concord hath Christ with Belial? Or what part hath he that believeth with an infidel? [16]And what agreement hath the temple of God with idols? For ye are the temple of the living God; as God hath said, I will dwell in them, and walk in them; and I will be their God, and they shall be my people.*
> **2 Corinthians 6:14-16 (KJV).**

Over and above saving us the trouble of being burdened by unbelievers, another important reason why God does not want us to take wives and husbands from other nations represented by the Canaanites as indicated above is, God wants us to have children who will glorify Him. Those upon whom His plan and purpose will rest. He wants children who will be dedicated back to Him just as Hannah did with Samuel, for Him to use according to His Will. Samuel became one of the powerful prophets of God because Hannah after receiving him from God dedicated him back to Him.

> *[24]And when she had weaned him, she took him up with her, with three bullocks, and one ephah of flour, and a bottle of wine, and brought him unto the house of the Lord in Shiloh: and the child was young. [25]And they slew a bullock, and brought the child to Eli. [26]And she said, Oh lord, as thy soul liveth, my lord, I am the woman that stood by thee here, praying unto the Lord. [27]For this child I prayed; and the Lord hath given me my petition which I asked of him: [28]Therefore*

also I have lent him to the Lord; as long as he liveth he shall
be lent to the Lord. And he worshiped the Lord there.
1 Samuel 1: 24-28 (KJV).

The above does not at all seek to suggest that only children asked of the Lord are the ones who come from God. All children are a gift and come from God irrespective of how and from whom they were conceived. The illustration merely seeks to highlight that God wants children to be conceived and born of couples who fear and revere Him and who will bring them up under His guidance and direction. In essence, God seeks Godly children.

[15]Didn't the LORD make you one with your wife?
In body and in spirit you are his. And what does he
want? Godly children from your union. So guard your
heart; remain loyal to the wife of your youth,
Malachi 2: 15 (NLT)

I believe it is clear from the above scripture that, God does not just want us to bear children, but Godly ones. Godly children can only be born from the union of Godly people. There is a reason why God wants us to conceive Godly children. He wants children who will be raised by parents who love and fear Him because they will grow to be God fearing men and women whom He will continue to use for His glory. This is exactly what God intended when He said to the man He created, "be fruitful and multiply".

[28]And God blessed them, and God said unto them, Be fruitful,
and multiply, and replenish the earth, and subdue it: and
have dominion over the fish of the sea, and over the fowl of the
air, and over every living thing that moveth upon the earth,
Genesis 1: 28 (KJV).

When you read the scripture as quoted above, God starts by saying *"be fruitful"* and then goes on to say *"and multiply."* In essence, God intended for Adam to first be fruitful or productive so that he can reproduce his productiveness. For us to be able to reproduce our fruitfulness, we must first be fruitful. If you marry an unbeliever, it will be very difficult if not impossible for you to be fruitful, meaning you will then reproduce what God does not want.

There are, of course, many people who bore children in sin (as of course we are all born sinners), and became born again and were used by God. Notwithstanding the latter though, that was not God's original intention or perfect Will. Albeit God did make a way for us to get back to the garden (Genesis 3:15), it has not been God's original intention for us to have to struggle our way back to the garden. God created Adam and placed him in the Garden of Eden to stay and remain there.

If you are not married, then you have a perfect opportunity to choose right. As already indicated earlier, love is a conscious decision that one takes. It is a choice made through exercising the mind power with the help of God. Do not be misled by your emotions and that butterfly feeling, and choose to marry an unbeliever because she or he is beautiful, handsome, good looking, wealthy etc. The consequences will be atrocious if you do.

Also remember that satan, the deceiver is watching you and will make sure he frustrates your ways so that you make wrong choices. If he managed to bring calamity to Job despite not having found any wrong in him, what more for you the child of God deliberately giving yourself in marriage to an unbeliever?

God wants you to bear and raise Godly children as indicated. However, it will be a difficult task to raise such children from a family that does not fear the Lord, let alone the one not believing in Him. It is God's plan that we raise our children according to His Will as this allows Him to continue using and having His way in them even after we have departed. I like the manner in which the NIV version phrases Solomon's wise advise.

> [6]*Start children off* on the way they should go, and
> even when they are old they will not turn from it,
> **Proverbs 22: 6 (NIV).**

I have underlined above the words "start children off". Although in the mind and plan of God, our lives start way before conception, in the human life and biology, the child's life and development starts at conception, not necessarily birth. Birth is just a manifestation of what has been formed nine months before. It is therefore important to "start children off" at conception before they are born.

Can one teach a child while still in the mother's womb? Oh yes, you can! A Godly couple can bless and prophesy the child while still in the womb, declaring for instance that this child is not a rebellious but an obedient child. A pregnant God fearing mother (and father) can every time as they communicate with the unborn baby, prophesy it, declaring how it will serve the Lord all the days of its life. How that unborn baby is in the plan of and is waiting to be used by God.

My wife and I have constantly being doing that and we are beginning to see the fruits with our first born son, Nsovo. It is amazing how he loves worship and praise songs even from when he was 2. The manner in which he moves and walks around when he plays praise and worship at home.

Although this is what he probably witnesses from me every Sunday during worship services, I do believe part of it is the result of us having introduced him to God way before birth through blessing and prophesying over him. The support of the father is also very critical at this stage for him to also bless the unborn child as the seed bearer. The Lord has even revealed to us already that the boy is a great evangelist and minister of the word even in his early years.

The experience I just related would never be possible with the unbelieving couple and very difficult in cases where only one partner is a Christian. It is for this reason amongst others that I believe God did not want the Israelites to intermarry with the Canaanites. Although God has already planned and orchestrated our lives in the spirit long before we were conceived, the authority and ability to bring these lives into the world has been bestowed upon us.

Yahweh, self-existent and all powerful as He is, chose to create man and transfer His creative power into the same man His hands created. Just think about this for a moment; He creates man in the spirit, sends him to the physical so that man reflects the nature, being, power, wisdom, ability and dominance of the Creator.

> *26And God said, Let us make man in our image, after our likeness: and let them have dominion over the fish of the sea, and over the fowl of the air, and over the cattle, and over all the earth, and over every creeping thing that creepeth upon the earth. 28And God blessed them, and God said unto them, be fruitful, and multiply, and replenish the earth, and subdue it:*

and have dominion over the fish of the sea, and over the fowl of
the air, and over every living thing that moveth upon the earth,
Genesis 1: 26, 28, (KJV).

You will note, brothers and sisters, that after creating all else, God made man in His image and then gave him authority and power to multiply and dominate everything that He had created before man. The above scripture highlights something very important. First, <u>God recreates Himself</u> in man, and secondly, He gives this man who is a replica of Himself, <u>ability to multiply</u>, authorising him to <u>rule and dominate</u> the world.

It has always been the plan of God to have His way in His creation, particularly, man. It is for this very reason that God recreated Himself in man. By recreating Himself in man, God wanted to dominate and influence the world through man. He brought us as kings in this world to reflect His Kingdom. It is for this reason that He first duplicated Himself in us before authorizing us to subdue the earth. With Him living in us, God would then be using us on earth to dominate and control the earth. As we continue to dominate and take control of the earth, He would in turn be glorified as we live for Him. However, It is also critical to note that satan, the small god of this world, had his own plans as well.

Satan specifically visited Adam and Eve before conception of Cain and Abel because he wanted to corrupt the seed, so that Adam gives birth to ungodly children. This is because once you raise ungodly children, it becomes easier for him to have his way in and through their lives.

Satan has long been in existence. When God created the heavens and the earth, he had already been thrown out of the realm of God. The darkness that hovered upon the face of the deep prior to the bringing forth of light by God, undoubtedly represented satan.

> *[1]In the beginning God created the heavens and the earth. [2]And the earth was without form, and void; and the darkness was upon the face of the deep. And the Spirit of God moved upon the face of the waters. [3]And God said, Let there be light: and there was light. [4]And God saw the light, that it was good: and God divided the light from the darkness,*
> **Genesis 1: 1-4 (KJV).**

Fellows, if God wants Godly children, as God's opposing force, satan on the other hand wants us to bear children who will be raised under his influence. His plan is to thwart the entire mankind from following and observing the ways and principles of God. It is without doubt that, if we give ourselves to the 'Canaanites' in marriage, raising and leading God fearing families will certainly be a difficult task.

I have witnessed several cases where marrying an unbeliever is justified on the basis that the person will either change or prayed through to salvation. More than often the person's natural good is given as an excuse. Some few years ago I was called in by this other Christian family to get my views on whether their daughter can be given in marriage to an unbelieving man. Over and above the gentleman being well off financially, the main reason given by the young lady was; "the man is good", "he does not stop me from going to church", "he does not drink or smoke" and "he does sometimes go to church himself".

Perhaps let me also emphasise that the young lady referred to above was herself a born again Christian. Despite my honest advice, backed by the scriptures, the lady was so adamant that she believed the man can change, particularly due to the fact that he even attends her church with her at times. She finally got her wish and got married to the "love of her life".

Although the above indicated couple is still married to date, the lady's commitment to the Lord has dropped dramatically, and it began to slow down subsequent to their marriage. I may not know what transpires in their marriage life on a day to day basis, however, what I have observed is that the lady's commitment to the Lord has subsided since she got married. This is exactly as the Lord warned the Israelites that giving themselves in marriage to the Canaanites would turn their sons away from their God.

⁴For they will turn away thy son from following me, that they may serve other gods: so will the anger of the Lord be kindled against you, and destroy thee suddenly.
Deuteronomy 7: 4 (KJV).

The truth beloved is that, darkness and light can never come together. Dating someone who is an unbeliever with the hope that the person will change can be a huge mistake. In all probabilities if that man who is interested in you reckons that your agreeing to marry him depends on him being of the same faith with you or being converted, he may convert. Not genuinely but in order to please you so he can lure you into marrying him.

CHAPTER 9

Take Time to know her?

If you are or were once a soul music lover and listener, reading through the above phrase would suddenly echo to your ears the breath of Percy Sledge pushing out that sweet voice accompanied by lyrics and melody that truly mastered how to captivate its audience. You and I have probably listened to, seen or at least heard this renowned gifted artist perform one of the beautiful and famous tracks of soul music, "Take time to know her". Unfortunately, this fallacious message from the song has been received as a true recipe for a successful marriage expedition, which many, from the class of the sixties to date, have probably fallen prey to.

If I were to give advice though, I would definitely come no short of ascertaining you that if you require time to know your partner, you better ask God to reveal to you how much time left your partner has to live, because knowing her will probably take you her or his entire lifetime from the day of your first date.

Let's once again revert to the Garden of Eden. In the process of providing a wife for Adam, God first sedated him. Upon the completion of the operation, God brought the woman He had formed out of man's flesh and bones to the man. All Adam needed as God knew, was someone who would come out of him. Someone who wouldn't necessarily be like him but complement him in all respects.

Surely, Adam was different from Eve in more ways than one. By merely being of an opposite sex, Eve was not like Adam in some respects, as much as she was like him in others. This may have probably provided a perfect justification for Adam to want to take time to know Eve. He was meeting her for the first time, after all. He did not know anything at all about her. However, rather than taking time to know her, Adam immediately connected with and embraced Eve, and in that way the first holy matrimony in the history of the world began.

Had Adam been a proponent of the 'take time to know her' philosophy, he would not have instantly acknowledged and received Eve as bone of his bones and flesh of his flesh. But that would obviously not have been possible! They were the first people in the Garden of Eden, weren't they? Of course they were! But weren't they also put there by God Himself? Now, if they were put there or rather were both created by God, who Himself recognised the need for their being together, how would they want to know each other? On what basis? From what premise would they be moving, because the very God who made them, is the one who saw them suitable for each other.

"But as the first man on earth, how could Adam have wanted to take time to know Eve, if she was all he knew since creation" – you could be asking. That's right; Adam was never exposed to other women before but to all kinds of animals. God had created animals and all that there was in the garden for him to enjoy and relate with. He put him amongst the animals to give them names. Perhaps he could have desired to want to know what different experience would Eve bring him, different from the one he had with the animals.

As the only human who lived at that time, and himself and God being the only persons he knew, what do you think he was doing when God was not around. Bored? I don't really think so! Adam related with those animals. He did not even know that there could be such a creature as different and beautiful as Eve. He could have found a companion from one of these animals, but none of them was suitable for him. After all they were just animals, and nowhere closer to being suitable for Adam.

> ²⁰*"He gave names to all the livestock, all the birds of the sky, and all the wild animals. But still there was no helper just right for him.*
> **Genesis 2:20 (NLT).**

What I seek to highlight from the above postulation is that, the partner God provides is good and suitable just for you, because He said so. She or he, requires no further scrutiny by you. If you yourself are able to give your child good gifts, how much more God?

> ⁹*"You parents – if your children ask for a loaf of bread, do you give them a stone instead? ¹⁰Or if they ask for fish, do you give them a snake? Of course not! ¹¹So if you sinful people know how to give good gifts to your children, how much more will your heavenly Father give good gifts to those who ask him,*
> **Matthew 7: 9-11 (NLT).**

As much as everything that the Lord had created was good, none of it was good enough to help Adam rule and dominate. None of it could aid him to multiply and subdue the earth. None of it could help him work the garden. On his own, he would have been fruitless than fruitful. God knew very well that it would not be possible for Adam to rule the world all by himself. By himself, Adam would not multiply.

When He created them male and female, God's plan and purpose was for a man and a woman joined in holy matrimony to display His nature and glory as they take control of and dominate the world. Upon realising Adam's need for a companion, God provided Eve, someone who was very well suited to help him manage the garden. In essence, Eve was brought to Adam already made suitable for him and him suitable for her. There was therefore no need for Adam to take time to know her and vice versa.

> [18]*And the Lord God said, it is not good that the man should be alone; I will make him a help meet for him,*
> **Genesis 2:18 (KJV).**

The Creator, who is all knowing could not have provided Adam with a wife who would not be good for him whilst He was the one who declared in the first place that He would make him a suitable partner. The fact that the only helper that Adam would get fulfillment and joy from had to come out of him as God noticed, attests that a God-provided partner is perfectly designed for you and does not need to be studied or scrutinised by you because she is from God Himself, taken from inside of you.

The question is; have you sought. Have you ever heard yourself asking God for a partner? If you have, what have you been or are you doing as you await God's provision? Do you spend time browsing the internet searching for that love? Do you attend every church conference, wedding and other events where you hope to bump into your bone? As indicated in chapter seven, that is not what waiting upon the Lord signifies. Once you pray for a suitable partner, whether you anticipate your marriage in five or ten years, get your tools in order, and work the garden. Your lifetime partner awaits you. God must first groom and construct you into that person who will be just rightly suited for her or him.

When we ask God for our partners, God does not scratch his head and go around looking everywhere to find someone good for us. He simply sedates you and removes a rib. Remember fellows, that the spirit is always active. Even as God has sedated you, your spirit must continuously be in touch with Him. As John teaches us, God is Spirit, and those who worship Him must worship in spirit and in truth (John 4:24, NLT). You continuously serve God while your partner is being prepared. Once the operation is complete, your bone will be brought to you, and surely you cannot want to scrutinise your bone. It's your bone!

Taking time to know your partner therefore is more like you wanting to know yourself as God gives us only partners coming out of us. Satan as indicated, will only seek to confuse you by bringing you a foreign partner. It is only when we begin to search for ourselves that he (satan) takes advantage and leads us to partners totally alien to us, most of which probably end up in divorces or very unpleasant relationships and marriages.

CHAPTER 10

Love does not love prematurely

In Songs of Solomon 2:7, King Solomon warns against arousing love before it so desires. Engaging in love prematurely robs people, especially young people, of an opportunity to fully enjoy their youthful lives. My friend, you are not living because you are in love, but you love because you have life. You first received life from Christ out of love, which warrants you living it in love.

God created marriage so He can display His splendor to the world. However, everything God does is perfect and orderly. God has designed life such that it has various stages, all of which must follow each other in their correct order. Just as there is time to be born, there is also time to die (Ecclesiastes 3:2). Similarly, there is time to love (Ecclesiastes 3:8).

It is also for this reason that King Solomon warns against awakening love before time. I indicated that all the stages of life must follow each other in their order. There is a time to be born, becoming a child, then a youth and an adult. Reading through the book of Ecclesiastes 3:1-8, reveals to us that for everything there is a season.

*[1]For everything there is a season, a time
for every activity under heaven,*
Ecclesiastes 3:1 (NLT)

The above scripture signifies that God has designed life such that every season will come at its appointed time. There are times in life wherein we need to be doing and focusing on certain things before engaging in love. As a child, you spend all your childhood development years learning how to live. You are taught so many things about life from basics such as brushing your teeth to greeting the people you meet along your path. As you grow older, you get introduced to more serious things in life, most of which have a bearing on your future.

As much as you are taught various subjects about life in school, which is knowledge you will most probably rely on for survival in future, there are other important developmental aspects such as issues of love and spirituality we discussed in this book. Unfortunately, these are not the focus of many curriculums. As we develop physically and educationally, we also need to develop spiritually. As indicated, although spiritual development is the most important, it is often one area that is most neglected. Prior to engaging in a love relationship, young persons need to serve God and rejoice in him in their youth.

*[9]You who are young, be happy while you are young, and
let your heart give you joy in the days of your youth,*
Ecclesiastes 11:9 a & b (NIV).

As highlighted before, love is a decision that has to be taken at some point. In other words, before engaging in love, there are other important developmental phases and seasons one has to go through. It is not really clear how long it took God to form Eve out of Adam's rib after creation. However, I believe that after creating the animals, the Lord God brought them to Adam not only for him to name but to relate with them as well. As we have learned, Adam still could not have a companion among the animals. Most interestingly is that when God was preparing a lifetime partner for the man, the man was unconscious. He was not even aware of what God was doing in secret.

> *"²¹so the LORD God caused the man to fall into a deep sleep; and while he was sleeping, he took one of the man's ribs and then closed up the place with flesh. ²²Then the LORD God made a woman from the rib [i] he had taken out of the man, and he brought her to the man"*
> **Genesis 2:21-22 (NIV).**

All that the man (Adam) focused on was seeking the kingdom of God and its righteousness (also see Matthew 6:33). While waiting upon the Lord, try to find the reason for your existence- your life's purpose. You are absolutely not an error. Why are you here? Why did God create you? There's a reason why you were born and probably made it through to this point where you feel fit and suitable to have a partner.

Perhaps you would understand this better if I were to put it to you that your existence denied someone else an opportunity to live. When the sperm that had been competing with millions of others to fertilise the egg in your mother's ovaries finally hit the spot, at that very moment you were conceived.

Let me attempt to put this into perspective for a moment. A woman was naturally created with eggs, which get produced in the ovaries. However, these are not really true eggs yet, and will never complete meiosis and become true eggs unless or until they are first fertilised by a sperm. Meiosis is a special type of cell division. Within the ovary, there is what is called, a follicle, which consists of one potential egg cell surrounded by special cells to nourish and protect it. According to biology, also called life sciences, a human female typically has about 400,000 follicles/potential eggs, all formed before birth. Only several hundreds, about 480 of these eggs will actually ever be released during the woman's reproductive years.

The point I want to emphasise in terms of the above is this; if out of 400,000 follicles or potential eggs, only 480 make it during the woman's reproductive years, then there must be something very significant about those that ever get fertilised. In essence, there is something significant about your existence. As you may know, a woman ovulates up to the end of menopause, which is often around 50 years or so. What this means is that, out of the 400,000 follicles that a typical woman has, 399,520 of them do not make it during her lifespan or reproductive years.

Now, try to give this a deep thought. How many children does an average woman today have? Roughly between 1 and 3, meaning out of the 480 surviving eggs if I may put it that way, only 3 at the very least will make it. This now gets more astonishing when one has to think of it in terms of sperm. Life science further teaches us that an average male produces millions of sperms every day. The average ejaculation during intercourse contains close to 100 million sperm. According to the World Health Organization, men who have fewer than 20 million sperm per milliliter of semen may be at risk of having infertility issues (WHO).

Now, look at it in this way; if the average ejaculation contains 100 million sperm, all of which will compete to fertilise just one egg, and within all that, only one makes it, surely my friend you can't view yourself as a mistake. Not even the worst of ignorance would justify your purposeless life. I believe that understanding the above analysis should be enough to convince you that before everything else, including engaging in love, you need to first understand your purpose and reason for living, because you are absolutely not an error.

In essence, your existence denied someone else, life. Let's assume that all the sperms that competed with you (the sperm that made it through to fertilise the egg) but never made it to this world, are given an opportunity to spectate your life. Just imagine how they would feel as they watch you waste your life, walking parallel what God has brought you to this world to do. Assuming that the sperm that made you was asked why it should be allowed to fertilise your mother's egg by God, then surely your reasons should have been convincing for you to be conceived.

The sperm and egg you came out of successfully completed the process simply because your reasons for why you should be sent into the land of the living were convincing and carried value. Indeed! You were predestined before the foundations of the earth. I'm only bringing this to show that even if there would have been an interview by the Godhead to determine who should be born, the fact that you would have passed the interview and ultimately born as you were, is a significant point that you need to grasp.

We are called to service (working the garden) prior to anything else. For some it could be ministry, others a particular profession etc. God did not create us for marriage but He created marriage for us. He did not create us for love but created love for us. Love exists to be exercised by us and not the other way around. We therefore have the power to open or not open the gates. Love does not love prematurely, but consciously and unconditionally. It is for this very reasons that King Solomon advises us to use this power correctly when he says; do not open the gates of love before it so desires.

> [7]*Promise me, O women of Jerusalem, by the gazelles and wild deer, not to awaken love until the time is right,*
> **Songs of Solomon 2:7 (NLT).**

Marriage is a gift that we come to enjoy while we remain in the place of our origin, which is God Himself. As long as we are in the garden, everything abounds. Indeed, because of one man's disobedience we lost our place in the Garden of Eden, but glory to the Most High for loving us so much that he offered us His only begotten Son, Jesus Christ, that through Him, we should regain our lost place in that Garden of God.

Jesus came to save us from sin, which had robbed us of our position in the garden. Simply put, by Jesus dying for us, God was restoring us back to Himself. Jesus sweated and laboured (work of the cross) in order for us to be restored back to that beautiful and glorious Garden of God. Figuratively, He brought us back to the place of our origin where we can serve and worship Him joyously in truth and in spirit while we wait upon Him to provide for our needs, including our suitable helpers. He is bound to provide you with that suitable partner, for He commanded that you be fruitful and multiply, which He knows you can't do alone.

As Christians, for as long as we remain in and continue working the garden, God automatically provides for us. When I said earlier there's no sweating in the Garden of Eden, I did not necessarily mean salvation renders hard work obsolete. Indeed, we have to work to survive but it was initially not God's plan that we should toil or do donkey work to make end meets. Working the garden was God's purpose for man, toiling only came after a curse as a result of man's disobedience.

> *[17] To Adam He said, "Because you listened to your wife and ate fruit from the tree about which I commanded you, 'You must not eat from it,'" Cursed is the ground because of you; through painful toil you will eat from it all the days of your life. [18] It will produce thorns and thistles for you, and you will eat the plants of the field. [19] By the sweat of your brow you will eat your food until you return to the ground, since from it you were taken; for dust you are and to dust you will return,*
> **Genesis 3: 17-19 (NIV)**

It is actually not Godly to work or labour for a blessing but a curse, as attested by the above scripture. The Garden of God was full of blessings and provision which man did not toil for. Love is a blessing, which is a gift from God and not to be labored for. Therefore getting a lifetime partner is a blessing (Proverbs 18: 22). You cannot work for or buy love. You simply serve the Lord as you progress in the other areas of your life, i.e. studies, work and business life, ministry etc. Your bone will therefore come at the right time.

When God decided to make a helper for Adam, He found him busy with the work He had assigned him in the Garden of Eden, an important aspect to understand. Once we prioritise God in everything, He will in turn provide for all our needs.

[33] But seek first his kingdom and his righteousness, and all these things will be given to you as well. [34] Therefore do not worry about tomorrow, for tomorrow will worry about itself. Each day has enough trouble of its own,
Matthew 6:33-34 (NIV).

CHAPTER 11

Love, a peculiar partnership

I believe by now it is much clearer to us what true love is, from a Godly perspective. That love which never fails but endures forever. Love that is patient. The one that regards not of its own, but of the other. Love that is not unconscious but unconditional. We do know that God is love and love represents God.

If love is God, who is so ginormous, then surely, it can never be fully defined by this little book. If God whose inexplicable and awesome nature cannot be reduced into this tiny book, then love remains an enigmatic process that can never be fully unpacked, yet will always be there to be experienced eternally. At least God is not going anywhere. He is and shall always be there to be experienced. Let me now add to the truths and revelations that have already been revealed to you throughout this book, another important element of love, partnership.

Relationships and marriage are all about partnerships. I believe that for any relationship or marriage to be successful, it needs to move from this premise. By engaging in love, you are in essence, venturing into a business or a partnership of some sort. Yes, a business or partnership of love. This partnership between a gentleman and a lady in love, is not just a partnership, but a very peculiar one. But a partnership is a partnership, how is this a special one"? Well, this is the kind of partnership I term, *"other-centred partnership"*, which is exactly what makes it peculiar.

In a normal partnership, partners do not just bring a certain contribution to the partnership, but are also conscious of what the other party must bring as well. Should one partner not be faithful to the partnership agreement in terms of delivering expected service for whatever reason, the other partner has a right to demand that service or even terminate the contract if not satisfied. In a true love partnership, however, the contributing partner does not focus and concern himself with what the other partner is expected or supposed to do, but what the contributor himself should be doing.

To understand the peculiarity of a true love relationship, let's for a moment try to unpack what a common partnership entails. Having noticed that people struggle to cross the road during rainy season, the municipality may resolve to build a bridge, after identifying the problem. Building a bridge would obviously require some expertise, which the municipality might not have. The latter then sees the municipality partnering with a company or service provider that specialises in building bridges to build the required bridge. After an extensive bidding process, the successful service provider is then appointed and enters into a contract or partnership with the municipality.

To ensure that each partner keeps their part of the bargain, there must be an agreement. To seal this agreement, a legal document in a form of a contract or the project charter has to be signed. The purpose of this legal document is to ensure that each partner does and keeps their end of the bargain. Both partners look forward to or expect some kind of benefit. Taking a project partnership as an example, both partners bring their share of responsibilities and commitment. This is to ensure that the partnership becomes a success.

The love relationship on the other hand, is a very special and unusual partnership. While partners in a normal partnership are more focused on what is in it for them, the focus in a love partnership is, "what do I bring to this relationship or marriage. In essence, rather than being preoccupied with wanting to know whether or how much are you loved, the question becomes, how do I want to love her or him?. When directors of the municipality sit down around the table to shortlist potential candidate service providers, all they are preoccupied with is, "what will this person/company bring to this project?", rather than "how much will we be offering him?" The focus is on getting the best qualified candidate who will perform an excellent job.

Similarly, the potential service provider will be thinking, "how much will I get out of this project?" rather than, "how can I ensure that I build a quality bridge?" Delivering a quality bridge is more influenced and determined by the benefit (package offered by the municipality) rather than by sole dedication of the service provider to deliver quality service.

Loving someone, on the other hand, is not determined by the returns or benefits due. In a true love relationship, the focus becomes more on how I want and intend to love, respect, honour, cherish, protect and serve my partner. In this type of partnership, neither party focuses on or is concerned about how the other party loves or respect them. The concern is not on what can I get out of this relationship or marriage but what can I put in.

It is not about asking a question, "will he forever love me?" Will she continuously respect me? Fellows, this is a very special kind of partnership that seeks not of its own, but that of the other partner. In a nutshell, as you anticipate your Mrs or Mr Right, attempt to first answer the question; "Am I myself Mrs or Mr Right?". It is important that you get an affirmative answer to this question because true love searches not for love but aims to give one.

Another unique feature of a true love partnership is that, it is not short-lived but permanent. By design, a normal project partnership has a closing or completion date, but the love contract doesn't. In other words, the project partnership only runs for a specific period whereas the love partnership runs forever.

Now that we have addressed how partners conduct themselves in an ideal love relationship, I would like to now provide a recipe to help both men and a women to work towards that admirable love partnership, which keeps eluding many. This is of course not meant to influence a demand of one attribute by one partner from another. The latter would actually portray simulated love. This recipe is meant to highlight important traits to be displayed by both partners in a marriage relationship, thus building a strong marriage partnership.

I have identified eight (8) essential traits or qualities that are necessary for a successful marriage partnership, which most marriages lack or are ignorant of (See table below). Two (2) of these qualities are at least shared. The traits can be highlighted as follows:

The quality of being a friend; the quality of being a lover; the quality of being a husband; the quality of being a wife; the quality of being a brother; The quality of being a sister; the quality of being a father, and the quality of being a mother.

In a marriage partnership, partners need to at least display the above indicated qualities in their relations with each other. As I indicated in chapter 4 in my endeavour to discuss God's philosophy of love for instance, lovers must above all be friends. This is the basis on which the relationship is to build. I have endeavored to demarcate the eight traits as follows:

The Husband ⇦ ⇨	The Wife
✦ You are a friend to your partner	✦ You are a friend to your partner
✦ You are a lover to your partner	✦ You are a lover to your partner
✦ You are a husband to your partner	✦ You are a wife to your partner
✦ You are a brother to your partner	✦ You are a sister to your partner
✦ You are a father to your partner	✦ You are a mother to your partner

The above analysis is solely meant to highlight critical personae that complete an ideal marriage relationship. It does not at all imply that you have to demonstrate all these eight traits on either side in the full sense. At least, the friend, lover, husband and wife attributes are more direct and can be revealed and exercised in the full sense.

Of course you are not a mother or father to your partner but your children. Similarly, you are only a brother or sister to your siblings, not to your spouse. The intention of this analysis is to demonstrate certain unnatural yet important traits that a man and a woman should somewhat display in their relationship with their spouses. As a wife, you can play a friend's, mother's and sister's role in your relationship with your husband. Similarly, the husband can be a friend, father and brother to the wife.

As I have indicated, it is critical that one understands this philosophy. It's quite possible to be the one and fail to be the other, which may lead to an unpleasant situation. For instance, you can be a lover but fail to be a wife to your husband or be a husband yet fail to be a lover to your wife. In other words all these attributes should be complementary. However we must be careful not to abuse the above philosophy. It is also possible that one element of an attribute can be misdirected. For example as a husband, you obviously can't want to play a fatherly role to your wife, but to your kids and the same applies to the wife.

Well, I guess the sisterly, brotherly and friendly attributes are quite easy to comprehend, so let me explain further on the motherly and fatherly attributes. The above analogy does not at all mean, you must literally play a father role to your wife and vice versa. The point intended by this analysis is that fairly in your relationship with your wife, there is also a need for some component of fatherly characteristics to play themselves out, for example to provide security (physical, emotional etc.) for your wife.

You might possibly get married to someone who grew without brother(s) and/or a father or to someone who has been abused by her father and/or brother(s), and as a result, developed that sense of insecurity that may have a negative effect on you, irrespective of how you may love or be loved by your wife or husband. In cases such as the latter, there could have been a void in your partner's upbringing. Please do not miss the point here, fellows. You cannot under any circumstances be a father to your wife as a husband, to the point that she feels like one of your children. Perhaps let me also share my experience in this regard.

Sometimes our personalities as men and fathers, lead us to behave in a manner that grieves and quenches the precious spirits in these delicate beings God has blessed us with. You need not be consciously acting as a father to your wife to an extent that she feels like you are treating her as a child. However, you could be doing it unconsciously. I have done it myself. It can be a very subtle act on your part that may somewhat claim responsibility to those perpetual conflicts you often have.

My wife is a prophetess. Even though signs have been there from the day we got married, I seemed not to have been taking it seriously. Indeed she is a prophetess, and has been one way before I knew she even existed. Actually, before she was conceived, God predestined her to be a prophetess.

Little did I know, that, my not realising this powerful and important gift in her, laid in the manner in which I treated her. I was actually the one quenching this gift all along, without even knowing or recognising it. But how? Well, good question. I did not realise that every time I raised my voice when emphasising a point, the more I was making her to feel like a child. This had a negative bearing not only on her as a person but affected the gift she has as well.

It was only when she raised it with me and said, "You know honey, I do not like the way you talk to me sometimes". "But how do I talk to you my love?" I asked. "The way you raise your voice at me sometimes. This thing is killing me inside. It makes me feel like a small child or school girl being reprimanded". Truth be told, I had no reason to defend myself, since I was not hearing this for the first time.

My mother, siblings and even some of my friends had taken issue with the same attitude before. There was therefore only one justifiable response from me, and that was to say, "I'm sorry". And of course, I did not apologise because others had complained about the same thing before, but because I realised I was actually not keeping to some of my marriage vows, i.e. to cherish and respect her all the time and in all respects, including in the manner in which I talk to her.

Over and above my apology and assuring her that raising my voice does not stem from a reprimanding attitude from my side, I realised I needed to change the way I address her when I disagree with her or make my point. You see fellows, this aspect of a fatherly trait was irrelevant to her but well-fitting to my little boy and girl. I had to repent instantly from that and glory to the Most High that by His helping grace, I relented and changed my behaviour.

The fatherly attribute has to play itself out at some point in instances where your partner needs comfort and protection. There may be situations wherein because of what happened in the past, your wife feels insecure. The reason she may be feeling insecure may not be because she is scared of you but that she still harbours the bad experiences from her childhood to this marriage. It is here where the protective and comforting role plays itself out.

One of the father's roles is to provide security for his family, i.e. wife and children. Remember now that as per the bible precepts, after leaving your mother and father, you took your wife away from her father as well and came to be one with her. What this signifies is that you somewhat took over her father's role of protecting and providing for her. In essence, her father is not there anymore to provide for her daughter but you are.

I have seen and heard most fathers in many marriage ceremonies and celebrations I have attended sternly emphasising to the groom, *"You take a very good care of my angel, gentleman!"*. I believe this father is not really exposing the poor man's inability to take care of his daughter or untrusting that her daughter will be well taken care of. The father actually laments the fact that her daughter will from now be out of his bounds and will no longer have him to protect and take care of her.

Similarly with the wife, she is somewhat a mother to her husband. Before the man left his mother and father from his minor years, he would continuously consult his mother before making important decisions. He would entirely rely on the advice and guidance the mother was giving. He always believed and trusted her mother's judgment when coming to major decision making. Just as he has now taken his wife away from her father, so has he left his mother to be one with his wife. In the absence of his mother, his wife now takes the role of his mother as the main advisor. He now has a mother figure from whom to enquire when he has problems and decisions to take.

I am not at all implying that his mother's advices are now obsolete. He still can consult his mother for advice but since he is now one with his wife, they now do the consultation together. First, he starts with his wife and upon agreement they approach his mother, who is now no longer a second, but a third party, for advice should there be a need.

It is also important to understand, as indicated, that it is possible to display one attribute and not the other, or to display other components of an attribute that are not necessary. For instance, a man can be a husband and fail to be a lover, just as a woman can be a lover and fail to be a wife. This aspect will be unpacked more in one of my subsequent writings.

There are many people who are bitter in life. But the fact is no one was born into this world bitter. Something definitely caused these people to have a negative view of life, which may most probably be attributed to lack of either one or all of the above figures in their lives. Unless this is well comprehended, it will remain a ticking time bomb hidden at the base of your marriage relationship, just waiting the clock to hit zero.

From the above analysis, we can agree that a display of all the indicated attributes sets one on a path for an ideal relationship. Is it possible? Is it real? Perhaps the fact that I reflect this type of a relationship as ideal, gives marriage pessimists grounds to view it as impractical and improbable. I believe not. If God's philosophy of love discussed in chapter five is anything to go by, then this is achievable. Of course, if one is to assess or put most of the marriages we find ourselves in today on the love partnership scale alluded above, the latter seems far-fetched. But it's achievable by the grace of God.

For me, at the heart of the definition of love as indicated earlier in this book, quoted from Corinthians 13, is the *other-seeking element*. I like it with the New Living Translation, which reads; "It (referring to love) does not demand its own way". In essence, love does not care of itself. It does not concern itself with what it deserves. It does not do and expect same to be done to it. Love always gives. It always puts the interest of the other first. Love always forgives. Not once, not twice or ten times, but seventy-seven times seven.

Love is wonderful, and it is one area I seek to learn and develop in, in each and every single day of my life. It should be everyone's duty under the sun, and I believe it was for this reason Paul said, "Let no debt remain outstanding, except the continuing debt to love another, Romans 13:8."

You are probably wondering, "Where on earth does all this exist?", "Doesn't it display a perfect world?" "Does this perfect world really exist?". Perhaps you are right. Maybe this is ideal. However, I do believe this is the perfection we can all strive for. No single individual can claim to have sailed through the above love partnership without any glitches. However, praise be to the Most High God that He still reveals His hidden mysteries to mortal man like you and me. It is revelations such as these that aid us to work towards that perfect marriage relationship God willed for us from the genesis of it all. After all, it reflects His very Kingdom.

CHAPTER 12

Journeying towards marriage

In my experience as a Christian and teacher of the Word, I have unfortunately come to a disheartening realisation that a plethora of God's children struggle to find references in the bible with regard to principles around relationships and dating. As much as it is not easy to extract specific steps one needs to follow in preparation for marriage, I believe God's Word does provide a recipe for this process.

As I already indicated in chapter three of this book, various church dogmas exist regarding what is considered the right way to marriage. Although it is not easy to find very clear steps from the bible in terms of processes that need to be followed in preparing for marriage, we do find examples of men of God as indicated in previous chapters, which we can emulate. It is very clear from the very first book in the bible that God is the one who gives direction in this area.

Without God at the helm, our pursuit for Mr and Mrs Right becomes a painful process filled with heartaches and sorrows. God has a plan about your life, hence, He wants to be at the core of your decision to engage in love. When

God said in Genesis 1:28, "Be fruitful and multiply", He was presenting His plan about a man and a woman, which was to lead useful and productive lives for His glory. This plan becomes clearer and practical in Genesis 2:18, when for the very first time in the account of creation, God saw something in the midst of His good creation as not good.

It was not the animals or whatever that was around Adam that God saw as not good, but his loneliness. As much as man was created in a male and female partnership in the spirit, so he needed to be in flesh as well. This would see the two partners display God's glory in the practical sense. In the flesh, Adam was therefore lonely and lost by himself and God was aware of that.

God values marriage very much as an institution that reflects His Kingdom and glory. This is why the devil goes against this institution with all that he has. Should you opt to get married, it is God's plan and will that your marriage be successful. It is through marriage amongst others that God wants to reflect His glory to the world. The book of Malachi conveys a very unequivocal message that, God hates divorce (Malachi 2: 16). It therefore could not have been in God's plan for your marriage to end up in the court of law. It is mostly because you may have missed it at a critical stage. That operation stage where God was supposed to perform a life determining procedure.

Take note that I said you may have missed it, and not God may have missed it. Let me highlight something very quickly. Any qualified surgeon can tell you that before any major operation, the patient on whom a procedure is to be performed must refrain from food for a certain period of time before the actual operation.

There are obviously various reasons why the patient must not eat before an operation, the main one being to avert complications. Now, should a patient lie when asked and say "I have not eaten", whereas they had a meal 15 minutes prior to the procedure, that may actually compromise the operation, including the very life of the patient concerned. In that case, the patient would be responsible for those complications and not the doctor. What I'm trying to imply here is that in order for God to be able to operate us so we can discover our bones, we also have a part that we need to play.

All that God requires us to do is to keep the doctor's instruction and refrain from food until the procedure. Wait upon the Lord. Adam, Isaac and Jacob did just that and eventually discovered and embraced their bones. Please revise chapter eight for what 'waiting upon the Lord' signifies.

Furthermore, understanding why most marriages end in divorce could very well be found in the analysis of true and simulated love highlighted in chapter five. It is possible my friend, that you are where you are today because your love was never real but simulated. According to the earlier definition, love never ceases but endures forever. Should you find yourself in the situation where you feel like you do not love your partner anymore, this could be an unfortunate revelation that, it was never there in the first place.

In all probabilities, you could have been engaged in simulated or faked love, the one that may have been blinded by certain features, physical or nonphysical, i.e. beauty, education, status, etc. It may be a hard one to swallow, but if you are honest, you will find that in hindsight, one of the above could be the reason why your marriage did not last. Of course it is not always that a failed marriage can be attributed to lack of true love. Getty's failed marriage discussed in chapter 4 provides a classic case in that regard, please revise. Let us now close by looking at steps or processes to follow from courtship to marriage.

Some years ago, I was invited by the sisters ministry in my church, to share with them about love and relationships. I was specifically requested to talk about the steps to be followed from courtship through to marriage. This is something I received with astonishment. Being entrusted with such a mammoth responsibility as a young person myself at the time, was itself overwhelming.

I had not been in a sermon or seminar on the subject before. Perhaps the obvious justification was that there was no reason for me to be in such seminars, since I was a young person not contemplating marriage anytime soon anyway. But why was I requested to share on such a difficult subject then? Maybe it could be that I often found myself at the centre of such debates as a young person at the time. But how could even that have mattered? I was inexperienced myself and could have only been misleading young people in those discussions. There was only one way for me on this one. To seek the Lord's counsel and revelation, especially since I was inexperienced, let alone not having spoken on the subject before.

The truth is, I did not want to mislead those beautiful young ladies aspiring to be someone's wife one day. I trusted God for the revelation as this is the subject that, although having scriptural reference, is not really obvious to everyone. This is a difficult process to outline, since various churches have conflicting doctrines in terms of how this process needs to unfold as already indicated at the beginning of this book.

We have looked at the fact that the scriptures are not clear on the specific steps or stages to follow from dating to marriage. Below, I endeavour to highlight what I deem a proper Godly way to follow in a journey towards marriage. The following table seeks to draw a distinction between Godly and worldly ways of preparing for marriage:

Godly Way (genuine love) ⇐ ⇒	Secular Way (simulated love)
Fellowship. In the process of interacting with each other, two young Christians attracted to one another have fellowship as the foundation of their relationship. Remember here the young Christians relate solely as brother and sister. Their interaction is limited by their service to the Lord.	**"Jolling".** Upon instant attraction, intimacies begin without any real interest of growing together in the Lord. The focus is much on the excitement and pleasure offered by the relationship at that moment.
Declaration and expression of love. The lover is certain of his choice and the beloved agrees to the love proposition, which gives birth to courtship. Fellowship continues….	**"Jolling" continues.** The lovers continue to enjoy the intimacy and passion brought by the relationship. They are possibly still exploring. The "take time to know her" philosophy is the nucleus of this kind of dating.
Courtship. Preparing and working towards marriage with time limits. The partners are certain. They approach the parents and pastors in their preparation for marriage.	**"Jolling" carries on till possible marriage.** There are no time limits. Relationship is just open to possibilities. When hard times strike, one party may easily pull out.
Marriage is not circumstantial. Their marriage is guaranteed and not determined by or dependent on any conditions.	**Marriage is circumstantial.** Marriage is not guaranteed and could possibly be ruined by circumstances.

Certainly, love is a choice. It is a decision that one takes based on a variety of factors. It is this decision that will determine whether you will experience everlasting sweetness or bitterness in your marriage. God is love and His love endures forever. If we place Him at the centre of our love relationships, we are bound to enjoy that everlasting sweetness and joy in our marriages. We will experience the beauty and joy of knowing Him even in the short term period we have on this puny blue planet.

I do trust and believe that the truths and revelations God has just revealed will go a long way in healing our society of these diseases of divorce and promiscuity that are plugging the world today in a bid to restore that God glorifying marriage institution. The very fruitful marriage that God willed at that point when He professed:

> *"Be fruitful and multiply; fill the earth and govern it. Reign over the fish in the sea, the birds in the sky, and all the animals that scurry along the ground*
> ***Genesis 1:28b (NLT).***

To God Be the Glory!....AMEN.

Printed in the United States
By Bookmasters